Overcoming Anorexia Nervosa

The aim of the **Overcoming** series is to enable people with psychologically based disorders to take control of their own recovery program. Each title, with its specially tailored program, is devised by a practising clinician using the latest techniques of cognitive behavioral therapy – techniques which have shown to be highly effective in changing the way patients think about themselves and their problems.

The series was initiated in 1993 by Peter Cooper, Professor of Psychology at Reading University and Research Fellow at the University of Cambridge, whose original volume on overcoming Bulimia nervosa and binge-eating continues to help many people in the USA, the UK and Europe.

Other titles in the series include:

Overcoming Anger and Irritability

Overcoming Anxiety

Bulimia Nervosa and Binge-Eating

Overcoming Childhood Trauma

Overcoming Chronic Fatigue

Overcoming Chronic Pain

Overcoming Compulsive Gambling

Overcoming Depression

Overcoming Low Self-Esteem

Overcoming Mood Swings

Overcoming Obsessive Compulsive Disorder

Overcoming Panic

Overcoming Relationship Problems

Overcoming Sexual Problems

Overcoming Social Anxiety and Shyness

Overcoming Traumatic Stress

Overcoming Weight Problems

Overcoming Your Smoking Habit

All titles in the series are available by mail order from Constable & Robinson Ltd. Please ring 020 8741 3663 for details.

OVERCOMING ANOREXIA NERVOSA

A *self-help guide using cognitive behavioral techniques*

Chris Freeman

ROBINSON
London

Constable & Robinson Ltd.
3 The Lanchesters
162 Fulham Palace Road
London W6 9ER
www.constablerobinson.com

First published in the UK by Robinson,
an imprint of Constable & Robinson Ltd 2002

ISBN 1-85487-969-3
ISBN 978-1-85487-969-1

Important Note
This book is not intended to be a substitute for medical advice or treatment.
Any person with a condition requiring medical attention should consult
a qualified medical practitioner or suitable therapist.

Printed and bound in the EU

10 9 8 7 6 5 4 3

To Aleck, my father,
the wisest man I have known

Contents

Acknowledgments   ix

Foreword   xi

Introduction: How to Use this Book   1

Prologue: A Day in the Life   5

PART ONE: A Guide to Anorexia Nervosa   7

1   What Is Anorexia Nervosa?   9

2   How Anorexia Nervosa Affects People Physically and Mentally   16

3   Anorexia Nervosa and Other Disorders   31

4   Anorexia Nervosa in Other Population Groups   40

5   What Causes Anorexia Nervosa?   51

6   How Can Anorexia Nervosa Be Treated?   69

PART TWO: A Self-Help Manual   85

Introduction   87

Step 1: Assessing the Problem   89

Step 2: Monitoring Your Eating   104

Step 3: Challenging the Way You Think, I: Automatic Thoughts   110

Contents

Step 4: Challenging the Way You Think, II: Thinking Errors 119

Step 5: Changing Your Eating Patterns 123

Step 6: Improving Your Body Image 131

Step 7: Developing Assertiveness 141

Step 8: Dealing with Anxiety 154

Step 9: Managing Your Relationships 161

Step 10: Coping Strategies for the Future 169

A Final Word 181

Useful Books 183

Useful Addresses 185

Index 187

Extra Monitoring Sheets 191

Acknowledgments

To all current and past staff at the Cullen Centre for Eating Disorders, Edinburgh, who are, and have been, a great clinical team to work with, and who have discussed and practised many of the ideas in this book. Particular thanks to Charlotte Nevison and Patricia Graham, who as psychology trainees did much of the spade work.

Foreword

Why Cognitive Behavior Therapy?

Over the past two or three decades, there has been something of a revolution in the field of psychological treatment. Freud and his followers had a major impact on the way in which psychological therapy was conceptualized, and psychoanalysis and psychodynamic psychotherapy dominated the field for the first half of this century. So, long-term treatments were offered which were designed to uncover the childhood roots of personal problems – offered, that is, to those who could afford it. There was some attempt by a few health service practitioners with a public conscience to modify this form of treatment (by, for example, offering short-term treatment or group therapy), but the demand for help was so great that this had little impact. Also, whilst numerous case histories can be found of people who are convinced that psychotherapy did help them, practitioners of this form of therapy showed remarkably little interest in demonstrating that what they were offering their patients was, in fact, helpful.

As a reaction to the exclusivity of psychodynamic therapies and the slender evidence for their usefulness, in the 1950s and 1960s a set of techniques was developed, collectively termed 'behavior therapy'. These techniques shared two basic features. First, they aimed to remove symptoms (such as anxiety) by dealing with those symptoms themselves, rather than their deep-seated underlying historical causes. Second, they were techniques, loosely related to what laboratory psychologists were finding out about the mechanisms of learning, which were formulated in testable terms. Indeed, practitioners of behavior therapy were committed to using techniques of proven value or, at worst, of a form which could potentially be put to the test. The area where these techniques proved of most value was in the treatment of anxiety disorders, especially specific phobias (such as fear of animals or of heights) and agoraphobia, both notoriously difficult to treat using conventional psychotherapies.

After an initial flush of enthusiasm, discontent with behavior therapy grew. There were a number of reasons for this, an important one of which was the fact that behavior therapy did not deal with the internal thoughts which were so obviously central to the distress that patients were experiencing. In this context, the fact that behavior therapy proved so inadequate when it came to the treatment of depression highlighted the need for major revision. In the late 1960s and early 1970s a treatment was developed specifically for depression called 'cognitive therapy'. The pioneer in this enterprise was an American psychiatrist, Professor Aaron T. Beck, who developed a theory of depression which emphasized the importance of people's depressed styles of thinking. He also specified a new form of therapy. It would not be an exaggeration to say that Beck's work changed the nature of psychotherapy, not just for depressions but for a range of psychological problems.

In recent years the cognitive techniques introduced by Beck have been merged with the techniques developed earlier by the behavior therapists to produce a body of theory and practice which has come to be known as 'cognitive behavior therapy'. There are two reasons why this form of treatment has come to be so important within the field of psychotherapy. First, cognitive therapy for depression, as originally described by Beck and developed by his successors, has been subjected to the strictest scientific testing; and it has been found to be a highly successful treatment for a significant proportion of cases of depression. Not only has it proved to be as effective as the best alternative treatments (except in the most severe cases, where medication is required), but some studies suggest that people treated successfully with cognitive behavior therapy are less likely to experience a later recurrence of their depression than people treated successfully with other forms of therapy (such as anti-depressant medication). Second, it has become clear that specific patterns of thinking are associated with a range of psychological problems and that treatments which deal with these styles of thinking are highly effective. So, specific cognitive behavioral treatments have been developed for anxiety disorders, like panic disorder, generalized anxiety disorder, specific phobias and social phobia, obsessive compulsive disorders, and hypochondriasis (health anxiety), as well as for other conditions such as compulsive gambling, alcohol and drug addiction, and eating disorders like anorexia nervosa and binge-eating disorder. Indeed, cognitive behavorial techniques have a wide application beyond the narrow categories of psychological disorders: they have been applied effectively, for example, to helping people with low self-esteem and those with marital difficulties.

At any one time almost 10 per cent of the general population is suffering from depression, and more than 10 per cent has one or other of the anxiety disorders. Many others have a range of psychological problems and personal difficulties. It is of the greatest importance that treatments of proven effectiveness are developed. However, even when the armoury of therapies is, as it were, full, there remains a very great problem – namely that the delivery of treatment is expensive and the resources are not going to be available evermore. Whilst this shortfall could be met by lots of people helping themselves, commonly the natural inclination to make oneself feel better in the present is to do precisely those things which perpetuate or even exacerbate one's problems. For example, the person with agoraphobia will stay at home to prevent the possibility of an anxiety attack; and the person with bulimia nervosa will avoid eating all potentially fattening foods. Whilst such strategies might resolve some immediate crisis, they leave the underlying problem intact and provide no real help in dealing with future difficulties.

So, there is a twin problem here: although effective treatments have been developed, they are not widely available; and when people try to help themselves they often make matters worse. In recent years the community of cognitive behavior therapists has responded to this situation. What they have done is to take the principles and techniques of specific cognitive behavior therapies for particular problems and represent them in self-help manuals. These manuals specify a systematic program of treatment which the individual sufferer is advised to work through to overcome their difficulties. In this way, the cognitive behavioral therapeutic techniques of proven value are being made available on the widest possible basis.

Self-help manuals are never going to replace therapists. Many people will need individual treatment from a qualified therapist. It is also the case that, despite the widespread success of cognitive behavioral therapy, some people will not respond to it and will need one of the other treatments available. Nevertheless, although research on the use of cognitive behavioral self-help manuals is at an early stage, the work done to date indicates that for a very great many people such a manual will prove sufficient for them to overcome their problems without professional help.

Many people suffer silently and secretly for years. Sometimes appropriate help is not forthcoming despite their efforts to find it. Sometimes they feel too ashamed or guilty to reveal their problems to anyone. For many of these people the cognitive behavioral self-help manuals will provide a lifeline to recovery and a better future.

Professor Peter Cooper
The University of Reading

Introduction: How to Use this Book

Thirty years ago, anorexia nervosa (AN) was a condition that few people even knew existed. In the 1970s it was called the "Slimmer's Disease" and was often mistakenly dismissed as an over-zealous bid to lose weight in order to be attractive. Since then, awareness has greatly increased, and more and more people are aware that this is a very real, and very distressing condition, and one that should be treated, not dismissed.

This book is intended as a self-help guide for those who suffer from AN, or who fear that they may be developing a disturbing obsession with body weight and food.* Part One sets out what is currently known about the disorder. In particular, it details the physical and psychological effects of the illness in the long term, from the effects of starvation on your well-being and future health, to the emotional factors that come into play when the disease takes a grip. This is not intended to alarm or distress, but simply to make you aware of the seriousness of the condition, to persuade you of the benefits of healing yourself and to offer some reassurance that you are not alone in your fears about weight gain and food intake. Part Two sets out a sequence of steps through which you can begin to tackle the problem. This is above all a practical plan, and is offered as a flexible framework, not a rigid set of rules. No two people with AN are entirely alike, so you may well find that some of the psychological techniques do not suit you, and you may wish to adapt some elements of the treatment plan. The important point to remember is that the approach described here has proved a useful one for many.

Introduction

In many cases of AN – particularly those where the illness is quite advanced – professional help may be necessary. How to go about finding the help you need, and what kind of treatments are available, are questions dealt with in Chapter 6 of Part One. However, self-help techniques can be useful even to those simultaneously undergoing professional treatment, and in such circumstances this book may serve as a back-up.

The book may also serve as a useful tool when trying to explain to those around you just what is happening to you, and what you are trying to achieve. AN is a complex disorder. It is both very public and very private. Much of the behavior is secret, and causes the person with AN a great deal of guilt and distress. It is also a very public statement of distress: the starvation state is obvious to all those around, even if apparently denied by the sufferer. AN has been described as an addictive disorder – the addiction being not to food but to food deprivation, to starvation. In many ways it is similar to addiction to drugs or alcohol in terms of the cravings, the preoccupation with the addictive substance and the withdrawal symptoms when it is removed. However, there is one major difference: the alcoholic or drug addict can conquer the problem by avoiding drink or drugs completely; the person with AN cannot avoid food, but has to learn to live with it and develop a healthy, relaxed relationship with it. This is not easy: very few drug addicts or alcoholics can reach such a state of controlled, relaxed use after a prolonged period of addiction.

This, then, is the task that faces you, your friends and your family. I hope that this book will help you through that journey. As you read on, please bear in mind the following points:

- I have used the female pronoun throughout, referring to the person with anorexia as "she" and "her", because AN is much more common in women than in men. I hope male sufferers will understand and not be put off. I am aware that men with the disorder can feel particularly isolated and alone.
- I have deliberately not used the term "anorexic" to describe those with the disorder. The alternative "person with anorexia" may seem unwieldy, but it is important to realize that you are not defined by the disorder; AN is a problem that can be

overcome, not your whole identity. Try to think of yourself not as "an anorexic", but as "a person with anorexia". There is at least a part of you that is *not* anorexic.

- Recovering from AN is not simple: there is no quick fix, no single solution. It will take time and hard work. Spend plenty of time preparing yourself for change. There is no need to rush things. Building up your motivation and strength to begin to change may be the most important step you take.

Prologue: A Day in the Life

"*My day began at 7 a.m. I never slept late, because I knew that I would burn more calories out of bed than in it. As soon as I was up, had washed my face, brushed my teeth and put in my contact lenses, I weighed myself. The bathroom scales had to be at an exact angle to the wall, on a certain floorboard, as I had worked out that this was the flattest part of the floor and therefore the place where I would get the most accurate reading. What I weighed at this point of the day was very important to my mood for the rest of it. You see, first thing, I couldn't attribute any weight gain to the weight of food inside my stomach or to water retention. It could only be fat. If my weight was up, I experienced a sense of dread. It was a terrible feeling, like being sent to prison. The rest of the world seemed to be blotted out, and all I could think about was this awful fact. These were the only moments that I really thought about the idea of getting help, because these moments were so terrible.*

"*If my weight was normal, I could cope, and so didn't consider trying to get help. If it was down, I felt a mild euphoria, which spurred me on to eat even less during the day. On days when my weight was down I almost loved my anorexia, because I felt like it was mine.*

"*Breakfast was my largest meal and it consisted of a plain, low-fat yoghurt and a sliced apple. From peeling off the yoghurt car-ton lid, and carefully licking off the yoghurt, to finishing the last slice of apple, I would say it took about 40 minutes. By then, my parents were up, and I was ready to make them tea and toast*

5

while I washed up my teaspoon and plate. I took the teaspoon and the plate from the table to the sink in two separate journeys, as this burned off more energy. I would do likewise with the tea and the toast, the milk jug and the butter.

"When I was finished, I would sit down and join them. With my mug of black tea in my hand, I used to congratulate myself on getting so far without being challenged. At ten to eight I began the walk to school, which took approximately 40 minutes, because I took a very circuitous route. Because I was in my sixth year, I had quite a lot of freedom to come and go as I pleased; I had a lot of free periods, having passed the exams I needed the previous year. This enabled me to escape from people at lunchtime – I simply couldn't cope with the remarks of my friends, who had become increasingly impatient with me. I would spend lunch-time walking the streets near the school and be back just as the afternoon bell was ringing.

"On my way home I would buy a small chocolate wafer bar and eat one half of it with a cup of black coffee. This had a laxative effect. My bowels didn't move otherwise. Afterwards, I did exercises. This was a routine of running on the spot, followed by sit-ups and upside-down cycling. I would work at it for an hour, with my bedroom door locked and the radio playing. I read in a magazine that you should vary your exercise routine as your body became more efficient at conserving energy when you did the same routine over and over again. This meant that I had to devise new exercises, including running up and down the stairs.

"The evening meal was usually Weight Watchers soup. My mother was always dieting, so I could actually eat with her, though I always said that I would get something else to eat later, otherwise she would nag me. After that, I would say that I was going out to visit friends, but I just went walking.

"I weighed myself last thing at night, to check that I was on target. I couldn't sleep otherwise. In bed, I would lie on my back and trace my fingers over my ribs and hip-bones to check that they were as prominent as they had been the night before. Since my periods stopped I didn't experience any pre-menstrual bloating, which I was pleased about."

PART ONE

A Guide to Anorexia Nervosa

1

What Is Anorexia Nervosa?

Anorexia nervosa is an eating disorder, especially common in – but by no means confined solely to – women. The disorder usually begins in adolescence or early adulthood, the mean age of onset being 15 years, but can start at any point between 6 and 72 years. If it does occur later in life it is more likely to be associated with severe psychological or physical disease (see Chapter 4 below). The central physical feature of AN is an abnormally low body weight, 15 per cent below that recommended for the age, height and sex of the person, accompanied by amenorrhea (the cessation of menstrual periods) in girls.

There are many physical and psychological symptoms secondary to starvation, but AN is principally a psychological disorder. Its characteristic feature is a fear of fatness, indeed fear even of existing at a normal body weight. This is accompanied by an intense pursuit of thinness. There is also nearly always a distortion of body image in which individuals perceive themselves as fat or overweight even when everyone else thinks they are grossly underweight. Other methods apart from starvation may be employed to maintain low weight, such as exercising, vomiting or purging.

Although clinical studies have shown AN to be more prevalent in higher social classes, population studies show equal distribution in all social groups, which suggests that there is a degree of under-diagnosis and under-treatment of socially disadvantaged people with eating disorders.

In some cases, what begins as a harmless diet escalates. Success brings with it feelings of achievement and control. Often, individuals vulnerable to AN are in circumstances where they feel trapped and under pressure to succeed; or they feel out of control in their lives. The reward they get from exerting control over their food intake and consequent weight becomes of exaggerated importance and may begin to dominate their existence. Chapter 5 sets out some of the factors which make particular individuals vulnerable to developing AN.

AN is one of a group of eating disorders particularly prevalent in adolescent girls. Also in this group are bulimia nervosa (BN) and binge-eating disorder. BN is characterized by constant dieting punctuated by episodes of loss of control. These binges may be very large, involving many thousands of calories, and are followed by purging, either with self-induced vomiting or laxative abuse, or a combination of the two. People with BN are usually within the normal weight range. Individuals with binge-eating disorder have episodes similar to those with BN but they do not purge. They may have periods of marked starvation between their binges. People with this disorder are generally in the normal or obese weight range. These eating disorders may exist independently and exclusively, but a person may have different variants at different times.

Approximately 0.5 per cent of the female population suffers from AN, 2 per cent from BN and a further 2 per cent from binge-eating disorder. If we include partial syndromes, which may represent those in the early stages of the disorder or those who are partially recovered, these figures can be doubled; that is, some version of these disorders affects approximately 10 per cent of girls and women. The sex ratio for AN is 10:1 female:male (no corresponding figure for BN has yet been established). AN also carries a substantial risk of fatal outcome: follow-up studies of severe hospitalized cases of AN show that between 0.5 and 1 per cent of these individuals will die of causes related to the disorder, two-thirds from the physical effects of starvation and a third from suicide.

These figures may be disturbing, even frightening; but it is important to remember that:

- Eating disorders are common: you are not alone or unique. On the contrary, many others share your problem.
- In order to prepare yourself for treatment, it is good to learn as much as you can about the disorder of AN and how it can be treated.

Some Common Myths about AN

Misguided, distorted and just plain wrong ideas about AN abound. Some of the most common are worth examining and refuting at the outset, because only with an accurate picture of the disorder can it be effectively tackled.

Myth: AN only occurs in women, particularly young women. It occurs in men of all ages and in women of all ages.

Myth: AN is a disorder of privilege, occurring mainly in the upper and middle social classes. It occurs across all social backgrounds and all levels of affluence. Clinic attendees tend to be from higher social classes, but out in the community people with AN are distributed equally across the whole range of social classes.

Myth: pressure or influence by the media causes AN. This is too simple an explanation. AN has multiple causes. AN is not simply trying to be thin to be more attractive.

Myth: AN is caused by families, by certain patterns of family interaction and by mothers in particular. This view, which is widely held, causes parents and daughters alike a great deal of distress and guilt. Most of the problems in families where a member has AN are a result of the disorder rather than the cause of it.

Myth: AN is caused by simple dieting which gets out of control. On its own, dieting does not cause AN. The majority of women have dieted at some time, and many have done so frequently. Only a minority get AN.

Myth: AN is not a serious disorder. It clearly is. In many cases it is very difficult to treat. The physical complications are severe and the death rate among the most seriously affected is high.

Myth: once you have AN you will never recover – you will always be "an anorexic". This is not true. Follow-up studies show that recovery is possible even after as much as 12 years of continuous severe symptoms.

How to Distinguish between AN and Dieting

AN is not caused by dieting. However, AN and dieting clearly do have certain things in common:

- Weight loss is the goal.
- To achieve weight loss, food intake is reduced.
- Exercise may be combined with a reduced food intake to increase, or speed up, weight loss.
- Calorie values are learnt and computed, sometimes quite obsessively, to the extent that the dieter/person with AN can remember the calorific values of all the foodstuffs she eats regularly without consulting a calorie guide.

However, despite these surface similarities, the differences are many and substantial.

Someone on a diet, as opposed to someone with AN, will generally:

- admit to being a dieter, and often be keen to discuss the diet, target weight, feelings of deprivation, lapses and triumphs;
- admit to feelings of deprivation and to having cravings for specific foods;
- feel a sense of satisfaction from achieving an ideal weight, and be content to reach that level and not lose any more weight;
- experience an increased interest in food, but try to steer clear of situations involving food so as to avoid temptation;
- not be competitive with family members in terms of reduced food intake, i.e. not feel defeated if she finds that she has eaten more than another member of the family;
- put their diet "on hold" for special occasions that involve eating, such as a birthday meal or a Christmas dinner;

- whether frequently or rarely, bend the rules of the regime, and not be unduly disturbed in so doing;
- not be very consistent: weight loss from dieting is usually uneven with a dieter losing one pound one week and three the next, or even regaining lost weight through excessive rule-bending;
- often fail: most diets are given up quickly and lost weight is regained;
- work to a schedule: diets are generally time-specific, especially fad diets that promise a certain weight loss within a certain time-frame e.g. "Thin Thighs In Ten Days", or regimes embarked upon with a particular end-date in mind, such as the departure date for a foreign holiday;
- have a reasonable goal – at least in terms of projected weight loss, if not always in terms of projected time taken to achieve it: thus some diets seem spectacularly effective at the time, but much of the lost weight will be fluid, not fat, and therefore quickly replaced;
- eat quickly in an attempt to satisfy hunger;
- avoid people who are eating indulgently, or even normally, as this enhances their feelings of deprivation;
- seek the support of others in her attempt to lose weight.

By contrast, the person with AN will generally:

- often deny being on a weight-loss diet;
- not admit to feelings of deprivation, or to craving specific foods, particularly of the high-calorie variety;
- tend to deny weight loss, and even attempt to hide it by wearing baggy, figure-concealing clothes;
- not seem to become distressed by the close proximity of food, but rather actually to enjoy it: many people with anorexia develop a great interest in cookery and preparing food for other people;
- strive to eat less than those around him or her: in the case of female anorexics, eating less than the mother and/or sister(s) is particularly important;

- tend to dish out unreasonably large helpings to other people at mealtimes; this may relate to the desire to eat less than others;
- be wholly dominated by the desire to be thin and the morbid fear of becoming fat;
- continually revise target weight downwards;
- tend to become obsessed with food – like the dieter – but, rather than trying to avoid things associated with food will seek them out, for instance by studying cookery books, visiting supermarkets and cooking;
- linger over food, chewing slowly and thoroughly, and trying to ensure that she finishes eating after everyone else
- tend to become increasingly phobic about eating in public, and may hoard food in order to eat alone and unobserved;
- see a distorted image, feeling fatter while getting thinner, and become increasingly sensitive and plagued by feelings of low self-worth;
- link self-esteem inextricably with perceived body size and weight;
- never break the rules – or actively fear doing so, and become deeply distressed if she does, whereas a dieter may treat herself to the odd indulgence and at worst be annoyed afterwards;
- tend to become very competitive and obsessional about achieving: exactness about mealtimes, calorie content of foods and eating rituals is mirrored by increasing obsessionality in other areas of life such as schoolwork and relationships.

How Common is AN?

The short answer is: Very common. Eating disorders appear to be occurring more and more often in Western countries, with severe conditions such as BN and AN affecting two or three teenagers in every 100 and reaching a peak of one in 100 among those between the ages of 16 and 18.

Unfortunately, some of those affected by AN do die as a result, most commonly from late-diagnosed infection, hypothermia, irreversible hypoglycaemia or suicide, rather than from the direct results of malnutrition.

2

How Anorexia Nervosa Affects People Physically and Mentally

This chapter sets out to examine, in some detail, the physical and psychological effects of AN, including serious and potentially fatal complications. This is not intended to cause alarm. Indeed, frightening people has proved a rather ineffective way of inducing behavioral change. However, it is important that you know as much as possible about what is happening to you, so that you can make an informed decision if and when you decide that you want to instigate change.

Physical Effects

There have been people with anorexia who have made a clear and informed decision that, for them, being thin is more important than halting the physical damage they are incurring, such as osteoporosis (bone-thinning), and the risks they are running of heart and kidney damage. On the other hand, there are many who, once they have seriously contemplated the harm they are doing to themselves, and the likely long-term results, have made a clear and informed decision that they wish to change, even though that means gaining weight.

At this stage, try not to dwell on the issue of weight gain, which is the greatest mental stumbling block to anyone with AN. For now, try to look only at the effects that the disorder is having on your body. Reading this information may even help to begin the process of thinking about your body in a different way.

Symptoms of AN

The symptoms listed in Table 2.1 are more common than those listed in Table 2.2. As with any chronic disorder, the longer AN persists, the more complications occur. There is also an increased risk as time goes on of major psychological disorders, such as depression, anxiety disorders and alcohol dependence (see section below on "Psychological Effects", and Chapter 3), which can make treatment more difficult.

The Metabolism

The human body is a masterpiece of engineering. When it is attacked by a disease organism, it creates antibodies to destroy the invader. When it is injured, it sends signals to the brain to indicate where it needs treatment. And when it is starved of nutrition, it seeks to conserve what reserves of energy it has in order to protect vital tissue. This is why, as you continue to under-nourish your body, the speed at which you lose weight will lessen. Basically, your body is adapting to "famine conditions", seeking ways to burn calories at a slower rate and so to preserve

---

Table 2.1 **Most frequent physical symptoms of Anorexia Nervosa**

Symptoms	Fatigue, weakness, feeling cold, dizziness, chest pains, heart palpitations, constipation, diarrhoea, amenorrhea (lack of periods), swollen ankles / puffy hands, cold hands and feet. If also vomiting, dental erosion (poor teeth), sore throat and a hoarse voice and heartburn.
Appearance	Dry hair and skin, pale skin, hair loss, lanugo (fine body hair), broken cracked lips, orange palms / yellow skin, green tinge to skin and swollen face.
Silent symptoms	Osteoporosis (thinning of bones), muscle wastage, brain shrinkage, impaired kidney functioning, immune system changes, ovary and uterus shrinkage, impaired fertility, anaemia, weakening of the heart muscle, low white blood cells (the cells that fight infection).

Table 2.2 **Less common physical symptoms of Anorexia Nervosa**

SYMPTOM	CAUSE (if known)
Easy bruising; bleeding gums	Vitamin C deficiency (most people still take sufficient vitamin C in their diet or they take vitamin tablets)
Gastric/duodenal ulcer	Stress; stomach acid not neutralized by food. Unusual; commoner in bulimia
Heart irregularities	Direct effect of starvation on heart muscle and electrolyte imbalance
Renal damage / renal failure	Chronic low fluid intake and dehydration; low potassium
Polycystic ovaries	Cause unknown; commoner in bulimia
Multifollicular ovaries	A stage the ovaries may go through during weight gain, when many eggs (follicles) may start to ripen at the same time
Brain changes	Direct effect of malnutrition (cortex of brain shrinks – can be seen on brain scan)
Severe muscle spasms and tetany (muscle tremors)	Electrolyte-imbalance
Purpura (easy bruising)	Starvation
Low body temperature leading to hypothermia	Starvation
Marked swelling of the ankles	Malnutrition; it occurs quite commonly during refeeding
Epileptic seizures	Electrolyte imbalance
Cognitive impairment	Starvation means the brain is poorly nourished and shrinks causing poor concentration, slow speech and slow thinking. Sufferers may appear to be demented
Sudden cardiac death	Very rare

your health. As your metabolic rate slows, so does your growth rate. In pre-pubescent individuals with AN, puberty is delayed; in women of menstruating age, periods often stop. The state of starvation causes feelings of fatigue and weakness as your body seeks to make you reduce physical activity and therefore conserve energy. In many cases, however, the psychological urge to increase activity and thus speed up weight loss will over-ride these physical feelings. As you seek to lose more and more weight, your body is actually pitching against you: hence that feeling, common to those with AN, that you are at war with your body.

Ultimately, if starvation continues, the regulatory mechanisms of the body will be over-ridden. Epileptic fits are not uncommon in people with anorexia, usually occurring in the context of a disrupted internal environment.

Some people who have been exposed to long-term starvation, whether voluntarily or by force, find it very difficult to learn to eat again, and remain chronically underweight. There are examples of political hunger strikers who, even after they have called a halt to their deliberate fast, have found it very difficult to resume normal eating habits and have developed a syndrome very like anorexia. Some former prisoners of war or survivors of concentration camps have never managed to regain the weight they lost, and have remained chronically thin. Such people often report that they cannot tolerate many kinds of food, or that they eat very slowly, and feel a marked bloating even after normal-sized meals. On the other hand, there are those who gain huge amounts of weight and feel a compulsion to eat as fast as possible and leave nothing on their plate.

Effects of Mineral Deficiency

The starved body will gradually become deficient in important minerals. This is due in the first place to a basic lack of nutrition, but is greatly exacerbated by vomiting. Lack of minerals can have very serious consequences for your long-term as well as short-term health. Lack of calcium, for instance, the symptoms of which include weak muscles and back pain, can lead to the development of osteoporosis. Young people with AN can be as seriously at risk from this disease as women in their seventies. A lack of magnesium, indicated again by weak muscles, can lead to tetany (muscle tremors), while a lack of potassium, indicated by feelings of thirst and fatigue, can ultimately lead to heart problems. And while excess salt (sodium) can aggravate high blood pressure and fluid retention, a deficiency can cause severe dehydration and dangerously low blood pressure. Those with normal eating patterns will take in sufficient sodium as part of their daily diet without recourse to the salt cellar, but as the person with anorexia has reduced her food intake so greatly, her salt intake will likewise be significantly lower.

The Skin

The skin may become dry and crusted due to starvation and low levels of oestrogen and thyroid hormone. Fine downy hair, like the hair on babies, may grow all over the body. At first this has a "peach fuzz" appearance, like the skin of an unripe peach, but the fine white hair can become quite long. This is called lanugo and is related to low oestrogen levels.

The skin may develop an orange tinge, particularly on the palms of hands and soles of feet, and on the rougher skin around knees, elbows and knuckles. This is caused by high levels of carotene in the blood (carotenaenia). Though it can be due to eating lots and lots of carrots, it is usually because the liver enzyme that breaks down carotene has failed due to starvation.

Muscle Wasting and Muscle Weakness (Myopathy)

When you reduce your food intake severely, your body turns first to its reserves of fat to nourish itself. There comes a point when there is little or no fat left to lose, and then your body exists on what little food it takes in and by metabolizing muscle. In extreme cases this includes heart muscle. You can literally be said to be digesting yourself. This muscle wastage results in a drawn and haggard appearance, like that of a much older person whose muscles are wasting as a result of old age.

The less muscle you have, the more slowly you will burn calories. Also, as the muscles are not getting all the nutrients they need, they often work even less well than would be predicted just from the wasting. Signs of severe myopathy are difficulty in climbing stairs or in standing up unaided from a squatting position, and a clumsy, flat-footed way of walking.

Low Back Pain

Low back pain in AN is common. This is not usually due to osteoporosis or bone thinning. It is often caused because the spinal column doesn't have enough muscle support, posture becomes bad and this puts strain on the spinal joints. Osteoporosis is a silent condition and doesn't usually cause any symptoms until the fracture occurs. With marked starvation, the discs between the vertebrae and the spine become shrunken and less elastic and this can happen to ligaments around other joints. Pain on exercise is therefore common because the joints are less protected and less supported.

The Brain

In advanced stages of starvation, shrinkage of the brain may occur. To try to keep the brain functioning properly, the body will utilize amino-acids usually reserved to form essential body proteins, further weakening other tissues.

The Heart

In cases of severe starvation, the heart weakens and its efficacy at pumping blood around the body is greatly reduced. Blood pressure becomes lower, which results in symptoms such as feelings of dizziness and faintness. In extreme cases, cardiomyopathy can develop: this is a condition characterized by the failure of the heart muscle to function efficiently, and can result in chest pains and palpitations.

The Kidneys

Low blood pressure, resulting from starvation, also has an adverse effect on the kidneys, making it more difficult for them to function efficiently. They can become damaged with persistent dehydration and also when there are chronically low levels of potassium in the blood (potassium is lost rapidly when someone uses vomiting or laxatives to control weight).

Gastro-intestinal System Changes

The whole of the gastro-intestinal system, from the throat to the rectum, eventually shrinks if the body is continually starved. This results in feelings of fullness even after very small amounts of food and drink have been consumed. Starvation also disrupts the activity of enzymes, active throughout the gut in the process of food digestion, and in bacteria growing more rapidly in the small bowel, leading to poor absorption of even the small amounts of food that are being eaten. Constipation is another common problem for those with AN, and can cause severe abdominal pain as well as general discomfort. It is often in dealing with secondary problems such as this that professional help is first sought, and thus it is from this point that AN is often acknowledged.

The Immune System

The immune system is responsible for defending the body against attack by bacteria, viruses and other agents of infection. In starving people, this immunity is very much impaired. The ability of the white blood cells to deal with invasive bacteria is reduced, the healing of wounds is grossly impaired (a problem exacerbated by a lack of calcium, which regulates blood clotting) and infection with unusual organisms, such as fungi, is much more common.

Temperature Regulation

When the metabolic rate is reduced, the result can be increased sensitivity to cold temperatures. Hypothermia is common among people with AN, partly due to hormonal changes, partly due to the loss of the essential body fat that we require to insulate us from the cold, and partly due to a resetting of the body's thermostat, which involves a part of the brain called the hypothalamus.

Someone with AN will frequently feel cold and tired, and possibly experience spells of dizziness.

The Reproductive System

Starvation impairs fertility by causing the uterus and ovaries to shrink. Amenorrhea (cessation of menstruation) is an inevitable consequence. If a starving woman does, against the odds, manage to become pregnant there is an increased risk of miscarriage, which is often the body's way of indicating that it cannot sustain a second life. If the fetus survives, there is a huge risk that the baby will be under-sized, under-nourished and subsequently liable to impairment in learning capacity in later life.

Energy Levels

For many people, the initial response to starvation is overactivity. Slowing down to the point of lethargy tends to occur only with severe malnutrition. For others, however, a lack of energy is experienced after even a small amount of weight loss. This variability is believed to reflect biological adaptations to crises. For instance, a high level of energy is greatly desirable when searching for food in times of famine, while underactivity, induced by a sapping of energy, is useful for preserving essential body tissue. Thus, some anorexic people develop a high activity level quite naturally, while for others it is a question of mentally over-riding the body's signals to preserve energy.

Physical Effects of Vomiting

Repeated vomiting eventually causes dental damage, caused by stomach acids passing through the mouth frequently, gradually eroding the teeth. Another effect is a constant sore throat, which may be prone to bleeding. Heartburn is also common, as a result of gastric juices, produced by the stomach in response to eating, having no food to digest (because it has been vomited) and attacking the stomach walls. In the long term, this superfluity of gastric acid can lead to the development of stomach ulcers. Stomach juices contain a lot of potassium, so it can also result in potassium deficiency.

Physical Effects of Laxative Abuse

Laxative abuse, another way of purging the body of food before it can be properly digested, strips the body of fluid, causing severe dehydration. It can also cause "lazy bowel syndrome" – a condition where the bowel has become reliant on laxatives to function, and so comes to a halt when laxatives are not administered. This can result in water retention, bloating and chronic constipation.

Are the Physical Changes Permanent?

The good news is that nearly all the physical complications of AN are reversible. Even the marked physical damage caused by very severe AN can be reversed – but only by weight gain, return of menstruation and maintenance of a normal weight. In 1996, a long-term follow-up study of nearly 200 women with an eating disorder was completed. In the cases of those who had resumed normal dietary habits and were considered "cured", fertility levels and bone health had returned to normal. However, this was a slow process, in some cases taking up to five to ten years after complete recovery from severe AN. The rate of healing is much slower than the rate at which damage occurs – for example, the bone loss which occurs over two to three years of AN may take eight to ten years to reverse – and there may in some cases be enduring effects.

Women who have had no periods for many years as a result of AN may return to normal fertility. However, young girls who have primary amenorrhea – that is, whose periods never start – may permanently damage their reproductive capacity and not start to menstruate even if they gain normal weight in their twenties. Some small studies have shown marked brain shrinkage in severely ill individuals with AN; while this is to a great extent reversed if normal weight is regained, there is a suggestion that a degree of shrinkage may be permanent in some cases. Most people with AN, especially those who also have BN, will require extensive work to repair the damage done to their teeth.

Overall, however, the body has remarkable powers of recovery; the important point to remember is that it is never too late to get better.

Behavioral Effects: Changes in the Way People Act

Changes in Activity

Many people with AN become highly active. They try to be constantly busy and on the move, and are often very reluctant to switch off and relax. They may exercise for long periods of time, or find excuses to indulge in calorie-burning activities, such as volunteering to fetch things, and therefore having to walk about or climb stairs, or setting out early to walk to a destination, rather than accepting a lift. Sitting still or doing nothing becomes increasingly alien to the person with AN, whose entire thoughts are focused on the issue of weight loss.

In some cases a person with AN may become compulsive about exercise, using it as a weapon against weight gain. After eating, and especially if the intake is perceived as excessive, compulsive exercisers work out strenuously until they feel certain the calories they consumed have been burnt off with activity. If for some reason they cannot exercise, for instance if they are a guest in someone else's house and do not have any privacy, they will tend to become nervous and agitated, even going so far as to visualize the calories converting into fat on their bodies. This can be an extremely tormenting experience for the individual.

When they are free to exercise, they will do as much as time and strength will allow. This may increase, as AN takes its grip, to the extent that physical activity dominates the day, and becomes an all-consuming compulsion. As a result, many people with AN have very strict and exhausting daily routines.

Other Weight-loss Behaviors

Other behavioral patterns associated with AN, geared toward weight loss and/or against weight gain, include purging, by vomiting or using laxatives or diuretics after eating, in order to rid the body of the food it has consumed. This is the behavior characteristic, as we have already seen, of bulimia nervosa (BN).

People with BN are more likely to have been slightly over-weight before embarking on a weight-loss diet, and tend to eat much more normally than those with AN alone. However, their diet can be extremely volatile, ranging from a normal weight-loss program to excessive over-eating followed by the urge to get rid of the food eaten, usually by self-induced vomiting. As the latter is done with the utmost secrecy, people with BN are not easily identifiable, especially as their body weight will gravitate toward the norm.

Consequences of Weight-loss Behaviors

Behavior geared toward weight loss such as starving, self-induced vomiting, laxative and diuretic abuse and excessive exercising may have profound psychological, physiological and biochemical repercussions.

- Psychological repercussions include violent mood wings, feelings of isolation and depression, and the steady erosion of self-esteem.
- Physiological repercussions include dilation of the small intestine, which can cause feelings of extreme bloating and further aggravate existing constipation.
- Biochemical repercussions include dehydration and an imbalance in the body's electrolyte levels. Dehydration, caused by the lowered levels of blood potassium and chloride resulting from starvation, can cause extreme lethargy and physical weakness, tingling sensations in hands and feet, and, if very severe, heart irregularities.

The Psychological Effects of Starvation: Changes in Thinking

AN is a disorder characterized by disturbed thinking. People with AN see the world very differently from other people, and their sense of self is dependent upon the narrowest of factors, namely, their ability to exercise control over food intake, and their consequent weight and shape. Thinking is further disturbed when the individual reaches the point of starvation, which induces a marked alteration in consciousness. Therefore, a person with AN who reaches the point of starvation must first gain weight before underlying psychological problems can be tackled.

In general terms, starvation will make thinking a slower process and short-term memory will be greatly impaired. In very marked starvation, the person with AN develops a slow, ponderous and rather slurred manner of speech, which makes it look as though she has enormous difficulty thinking and speaking at the same time. She will often have a "punch-drunk" appearance, characterized by a vagueness of facial expression and an inability to focus. These changes are believed to be caused by starvation affecting the frontal lobes of the brain. These exert an executive function over the rest of the brain, and provide the fine-tuning to personality, controlling such processes as judgment, making choices and giving emotional expression.

The inevitable consequences of the starvation state include poor concentration, indecisiveness, anxiety, emotional instability, social withdrawal and lack of libido (though many anorexics avoid sexual relations because they have such a low opinion of their personal attractiveness). Each of these develops slowly, but over time they will become noticeable and effect a definite alteration in personality.

The marked changes caused by severe starvation both in the way a person thinks and in how she regards herself in relation to the world can be categorized as follows.

Preoccupation with Food

The most striking change in someone with AN is, of course, the person's preoccupation with food, which becomes involuntary and dominates not just conscious thought, but feelings and dreams. Ruminations regarding food that has already been consumed and food that is to be consumed prevail. Recipes may be collected and pored over, and many people with AN develop a love of shopping for food, cooking and preparing food for others (their own is prepared and eaten separately). This over-riding preoccupation with food reduces the person's scope of thought and experience enormously.

A person with AN may become an extraordinarily picky eater, and develop extremist food fads that exasperate those around them. Vegetarianism is especially common, and may take a particularly strict form, with an insistence on vegetarian cheese and gelatin-free products. This not only adds extra complica-tions to the whole business of eating, it also rules out many foods and therefore equips the person with extra reasons to refuse to eat. A vegan diet offers even more food-refusal possibilities.

The action of eating tends, in itself, to become very ritualized. This is partly a ploy on the part of the anorexic to mask a reduced food intake, and partly a way to draw out the event. This ritualization may include eating very slowly, and chewing each mouthful a set number of times; eating items of food in a particular order; cutting food up into tiny pieces before commencing eating.

Social occasions that revolve around food are dreaded by the person with AN, as spontaneous eating, governed by appetite, has become alien by the time the disorder has taken a serious hold. The person with AN is panic-stricken about the possibility of losing self-control, and thus over-eating, and also about the possibility of being pressurized by others to over-eat. Unfortu-nately for those with AN, food plays a huge role in our society and its celebrations. Occasions from birthdays to job promo-tions to holy festivals are all celebrated by eating in larger quan-tities than normal. Food is also the commonest thing with which we reward children who have behaved well and is also the means by which we comfort those in distress. As we are brought up this way, we become strongly inclined to use food as a treat or com-fort, for ourselves and our friends and family, when we become adults. For most people this is not a problem, but for the person with AN it can become a nightmare. Not only must she make excuses as to why her portion is tinier than everyone else's at functions and parties, she must also find excuses for abstaining when the box of chocolates is passed round the office or a friend turns up at the door with a birthday cake.

What may begin as merely the avoidance of food can eventually have dramatic and devastating effects on personal relationships. The person with AN may be able to cope for a certain length of time, but ultimately she will find the effort of resisting the temptations and pressures attendant upon such occasions leads to hostility toward other people and avoidance of such events. Those around her, be they colleagues, family members or friends, will feel hurt and bewildered by this behavior, and this in turn will increase her feelings of isolation and loneliness, allowing the disease to develop an even greater dominance.

Rigidity

Starvation causes thinking to become very rigid and inflexible. This is what is commonly referred to as "black-and-white thinking", where a person can distinguish only between extremes of right and wrong, good and bad, nice and horrible, and loses the ability to distinguish shades of meaning. This greatly hampers the capacity to think in abstract terms; the starving person can work only with very concrete ideas. Amenability to rational argument is also greatly reduced: the mind refuses to entertain ideas and concepts other than its own, and as a result, many find trying to reason with a person affected by anorexia a pointless process.

Immature Thinking

There is in AN a reversion to an immature system of thinking which involves the person believing that she is immune to the principles that govern other people's lives. For example, if an adult tells a seven-year-old boy that, in 10 years' time, he will be more than happy to kiss girls, he will both believe and not believe what the adult says. He will accept that 17-year-old boys like to kiss girls, probably because he has witnessed such things, but he will not accept that he will behave the same way when he is 17. Similarly, someone with AN will accept that, yes, anorexia nervosa is an illness that distorts the way a person sees herself, but will not accept that it affects her in this way.

Obsessionality

AN brings an increase in obsessionality. This is not restricted to thoughts of and behavior around food; it can affect many areas. There may develop a compulsion toward neatness and order, punctuality and cleanliness. These obsessions can cause the individual's day to be packed with time-consuming rituals, from folding down the sheets of the bed in a certain way to showering before and after meals or exercise. They may even serve as a way of keeping activity levels high. However, in some cases, the person with AN may excuse herself entirely from these rules and instead, impose them on other people – becoming intolerant, for example, of people who are late, or make a mess, or refuse to finish the food that is on their plate. In short, the person with anorexia has become unable to cope with those who do not cater to these obsessions, and this can increase the sense of isolation she feels, and the sense of frustration and helplessness felt by those around her.

Stereotyped Thinking and Behavior

This refers to doing and saying the same things over and over again, such as constantly asking for reassurance and repeating phrases and rituals. This kind of thinking makes it almost impossible for the person with AN to progress from one thought or idea, and thus during an argument they will be unable to develop ideas or defences, as they would were they not starving. People often describe arguments with anorexics as being like going round in ever-decreasing circles. As the illness takes hold, it seems to squeeze out the ability to think, so that the frame of reference and any development from it becomes smaller and smaller.

3

Anorexia Nervosa and
Other Disorders

Anorexia and Bulimia

Anorexic behavior exists on a continuum between the two extremes of absolute abstinence and bulimia. (For more information on BN and binge-eating disorder, see Peter Cooper's book in this series, *Bulimia Nervosa and Binge Eating*.) The eating patterns of the person with abstinent AN involve severely restricting food intake, and closely monitoring and pursuing thinness. Typically, all foods considered fattening, such as carbohydrates and fats, are banned and bulky, low-calorie foods, such as vegetables and fruit, are allowed.

If the individual exists in a state of starvation for a sufficient length of time, the rigid diet may be broken by a desperate eating binge in which everything and anything available is eaten rapidly. In such an episode food may be eaten straight from tins, insufficiently defrosted from the freezer – whatever is to hand, without thought as to its calorie content or appetizing nature. The food is usually eaten extremely quickly, without being enjoyed and frequently without being properly chewed and digested. This kind of episode is called a bulimic episode, as it is followed by feelings of self-loathing and disgust, which prompt the person to rid herself of the food as quickly as possible. She may do this by self-induced vomiting or by taking a large quantity of laxatives, in order to get rid of the food before the calories have been absorbed. Between 40 and 50 per cent of people with AN experience bulimic episodes.

Bulimic AN is a different story from "pure", abstinent anorexia, and is characterized by feelings of guilt, self-disgust and failure. It is also self-abusive, in that the person often regards the post-binge purging as a form of self-punishment. In contrast to the control and perfectionism of AN, BN tends to be associated with impulsivity, and can include or lead to such behaviors as alcohol or drug abuse, sexual promiscuity or stealing. The feelings of self-disgust experienced by the person with BN may reach the extremes of self-harm, such as body-cutting or burning, and may prompt suicide attempts. The behavior of the person with BN, characterized by high impulsivity, emotional instability, explosive relationships and self-destructive tendencies, is similar to the condition of borderline personality disorder.

The concept of addiction is also closely related to the behavior of the person with BN, as the binges are compulsive and secretive, and the individual comes to rely on them as a comfort, or escape hatch, when they find themselves unable to deal with life's problems.

"I had to have a 'perfect' day, in terms of eating, or it would end with a binge. Some days I knew in the morning that I would go home and do it, and I would stop in at the supermarket on the way home to stock up. Everything would be ready-to-eat, and I would buy things that normally I would never allow myself, things like pies, chocolate and always ice-cream. I always made sure I had a 2 litre bottle of lemonade as well, as it made the process of vomiting much easier afterwards. While I was eating I felt kind of high, but as I began to feel full to bursting point, the panic would set in. As soon as the binge was finished, I would go to the bathroom and begin to make myself sick. This involved putting my fingers down my throat, and sometimes taking gulps of water from the tap to help the food come up. When I was done, I felt quite light-headed and sort of cleansed."

Lucy

The two forms of AN, abstinent and bulimic, are not mutually exclusive. As mentioned, the abstainer will occasionally have bouts of bingeing and the person with BN will have episodes of self-starvation. However, if the patient is more bulimic than abstinent, her body weight will be nearer to normal than that of the abstainer, and she will therefore find it easy to keep the behavior secret. In pursuit of this secrecy, people with BN often purchase the food they intend to binge on separately, and hide the evidence from others. Those with abstinent AN are far easier to detect as their bodies shows the symptoms of the illness.

Whatever the primary behavior type, at the core of AN is the individual's fear of gaining weight, and her efforts to avoid this.

AN and Other Psychological Disorders

Although the "classical" picture of AN is now widely recognized, the disorder often merges into and overlaps with many other psychological conditions. For more information on these, including those mentioned in the following paragraphs, see other books in this series listed in the Useful Books section on p. 183 below.

AN and Depression

When using the term "depression" here, we are not just referring to everyday sadness and unhappiness. The qualities which go to make up what psychiatrists would call a depressive illness or major depressive disorder include persistent low mood or lack of feelings; sleep disturbance; lack of energy; poor memory; poor concentration; feelings of guilt and worthlessness; and a very negative or pessimistic view of yourself, your past and the world around you. Sufferers say they feel empty or dead inside; it is as though their feelings were paralysed. Many cultures have a quite different set of words to describe this feeling – in the nineteenth century we used the word "melancholia" – but unfortunately in contemporary Western society we use the word "depression" to cover a wide range of feelings from mild, brief unhappiness to persistent and all-embracing despair.

Low mood, persistent depression and depressive illness often coexist with AN. The relationship is a complex one. Some people quite rapidly get "dieting depression" when they go on a strict diet – indeed, their mood may drop even before any significant weight loss has occurred. Others get the opposite reaction and may experience a marked sense of elation, increased energy and well-being when they first embark on a diet. At some stage almost all people who are in a state of severe starvation will get depressed. Sometimes this is a gradual process, the depression getting deeper and deeper the more marked the weight loss; sometimes it can be quite sudden. I have one patient who seems to be fine until her weight drops below 40kg (88lb). At 42kg (93lb) she can be cheerful, bubbly and full of energy, but at 39 kg (86lb) she is physically and mentally slowed up, has a very pessimistic view of herself and the world around her, and experiences major symptoms of depression. This depression does not respond to anti-depressant drugs or to psychotherapy but is dispelled by a small amount of weight gain.

In other individuals the weight loss can be extremely severe before depression sets in. Very occasionally, individuals who have starved themselves close to the point of death (23–4kg or 50–3lb) still appear quite cheerful. However, in these individuals the apparently happy mood is often very brittle and may hide a great deal of personal pain and distress. In these cases there seems a clear relationship between low mood and the starvation state.

In some individuals it appears that the depression may have come first. Many women whose AN began in adolescence can in retrospect identify a clear period of depression over a few weeks or months before they started dieting. It was almost as though their dieting was a response to their low mood, and sometimes a partial solution to it. When they came for treatment there was no sign of the depression at all; but when they recovered from their AN either they were able to remember and recognize the depressive period they'd had, or, more distressingly, their depression came back when they gave up their anorexic coping mechanisms.

A third pattern is when depression occurs after many years of AN symptoms. Depression is a common occurrence in many chronic and disabling disorders, and it is difficult to establish whether there is anything special or different about the depression that occurs in chronic AN compared with that which may occur in someone with a chronic physical condition such as rheumatoid arthritis, epilepsy or diabetes. The depression may be a result of having to cope with a serious disabling disorder which affects all aspects of your life.

In a fourth situation AN and depression occur simultaneously. This is particularly distressing because the individual is beset at the same time by two equally disabling and painful conditions. One positive aspect, however, is that people in this group do tend to seek help early.

Figure 3.1 **Elements of AN and other psychological symptoms**

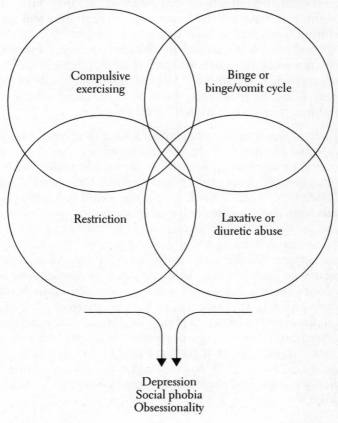

35

AN and Obsessional Disorders

An obsession is a repeated, intrusive thought that comes into your mind against your will, and that is difficult or impossible to resist. Usually there is a need to do or think something to neutralize or counteract the thought. Compulsions are the rituals that people carry out in response to their obsessional thoughts. Examples are counting, touching, washing and checking rituals. Obsessional thoughts may revolve around themes such as fear of contamination, fear of being harmed or harming others, the need for order or symmetry, or the need to feel clean or to feel things are "just right". These thoughts are not hallucinations. Obsessional individuals do not hear voices; they know the thoughts they have are their own, even though they feel alienated from them and do their best to resist them.

AN and obsessive–compulsive disorder overlap in two areas. First, many of the core symptoms of AN have a definite obsessional quality to them. The repeated thoughts about food, fatness, body shape and size fit all the criteria for obsessional symptoms. The case of Richard is an example.

> Richard was a 19-year-old student with a three-year history of AN. His diet had become extremely restricted so that he could only eat white food off large white plates. The plates had to be scrupulously clean and he had to wash them several times before they could be used; no one else could touch the plate. His main diet consisted of boiled white fish. He would boil the fish in plain unsalted water and stand over the pan with a paper towel, dabbing the globules of oil and fat which rose to the surface. The fish would be boiled until it was mush; then it would be "safe" to eat. Although much of his behavior was about avoiding calories, eating mainly protein and particularly avoiding fat, there was a definite "magical", ritualistic quality to it. The whiteness clearly symbolized purity and cleanliness, and was seen as good. He was not particularly afraid of germs; it was just that the food had to feel and look right before he could eat it. Richard's obsessionality got worse the thinner he got, and largely disappeared when he recovered from his AN.

Second, about half of all individuals with AN develop obsessional thoughts in areas not directly related to food. They have quite separate checking, counting or touching rituals or a repeated need for order, symmetry or having things feel "just right". The case of Jane is an example.

Jane is a 32-year-old woman who has clear symptoms of both AN and obsessive–compulsive disorder. Many of her obsessions, but not all of them, revolve around food. She takes three hours to prepare her evening meal, even though she ends up eating virtually the same every night. She has to weigh and check things repeatedly, and the meal has to feel and look just right before she can eat it. She is constantly on the move; while she is preparing food she goes backwards and forwards between the kitchen and the living room, deliberately only taking one thing at a time. When she moves round the kitchen she always takes the longest distance between two points. These are ways of keeping moving and burning off calories. She lives in a second-floor flat and has to climb up and down the stairs at least 10 times each evening before she can feel satisfied. She will always find a rational reason for this but knows that she is quite driven. She eventually sits down exhausted about 9 p.m. in front of the TV to eat her meal and allows herself an hour of relaxation.

Jane's other obsessions include cleanliness and tidiness. She cleans the house every day when she gets home from work and tidies it up, even though she lives alone and the room has remained untouched since she left it that morning. Some of these activities obviously also involve exercise, but others are to do with order and symmetry: these include having all the book spines on the book shelf even, the magazines neatly arranged, the ornaments on the mantelpiece positioned in an exactly symmetrical way and the pictures all checked to see that they are straight.

Jane's hands are red, raw and scaly from repeated washing, and the cuticles around her fingernails are all inflamed.

Jane has no time for any social or recreational activities; work, food preparation, exercising and cleaning take up 19 hours a day. She gets approximately five hours sleep.

For a person to be diagnosed with obsessive–compulsive disorder requires more than simply being obsessed or preoccupied. People may be obsessed with books or model railways or animal welfare and spend a great deal of time thinking about their subject; however, in most cases there is no sense of resistance, the activities are often pleasurable or give a sense of satisfaction, and there is no sense that by carrying out some sort of ritual you will magically alter what has been done.

AN and Anxiety Disorders

Anxiety is a very common symptom in individuals with AN and has multiple triggers. There is anxiety about food, eating, body shape, the need to exercise and feelings of being out of control.

More specific anxiety symptoms can be seen in a number of areas:

- *Social anxiety about eating.* Many people with AN find eating in company very stressful. They prefer to eat alone, they hate being observed while they're eating, and they find eating with strangers worst of all. This can escalate into a severe social phobia where eating in public seems absolutely impossible.
- *Social anxiety about appearance.* This too can become severe, leading to very withdrawn and isolating behavior. Beset by feelings of disgust with her appearance, convinced that she is fat and repulsive, the individual does not want to be seen at all. Some people become virtually housebound, going out only early in the morning or late at night, covering their faces with long hair and wearing bulky, loose-fitting clothes to hide their appearance completely.
- *Agoraphobia.* In our experience this is not common in women with AN. Whereas social anxiety refers to a fear of being observed or scrutinized, agoraphobia is a fear of open spaces, of being far from home, of being trapped in a crowd or stuck in an elevator. So agoraphobia refers to a fear of the situation rather than fear of the individuals within it. AN sufferers seem much more concerned with the judgments and appraisals of

others, and often feel relatively more relaxed when they are in a crowd and anonymous.

- *Anxiety leading to panic attacks.* In contrast, these are common. A panic attack is where anxiety escalates rapidly and one feels overwhelmed by feelings of anxiety, sweating, rapid heartbeat and dizziness. Often this is associated with rapid breathing (hyperventilation).

For more information on anxiety disorders and how to cope with them, see the books in this series by Helen Kennerley, *Overcoming Anxiety*, and Gillian Butler, *Overcoming Social Anxiety and Shyness*.

4

Anorexia Nervosa in Other Population Groups

Anorexia in Children

As discussed in Chapter 1, AN usually begins in adolescence; however, it is now known that AN can be identified in children as young as six, and such childhood cases of AN are being increasingly reported. Since diagnosis of AN in children has been quite rare and controversial, care must be taken to rule out the presence of another primary causal condition. Perhaps in part as a result of such caution, diagnosis of AN in children is frequently delayed. This is highly unfortunate, for the condition can have devastating effects if undetected in pre-pubescent children, permanently damaging growth and development; early diagnosis and competent treatment are vital.

The incidence of childhood AN is not known; however, it has become clear that, while the disorder is less common in children than in adolescents or adults, the numbers are rising. A common finding with childhood AN is the relatively high percentage of boys who have the disorder. In adults with AN, men account for only 5–10 per cent of cases, whereas in children boys have been reported to account for between 20 and 25 per cent. It is not yet clear if this is a definite gender difference or whether younger boys are simply more likely to come to medical attention than girls of the same age. One interesting difference has emerged in that while the girls tend to say they want to be thin for aesthetic reasons, the boys often give reasons of health and fitness.

What are the Main Differences Between AN in Children and AN in Adolescents?

Physical deterioration is more rapid in children, possibly because they have less fatty tissue in their bodies. However, this may appear to be a problem of growth or failure to reach puberty, rather than the more obvious weight loss characteristic of adolescent AN. Depressive symptoms appear earlier and more commonly in childhood AN, possibly as a result of the faster rate of deterioration, and anorexic symptoms escalate with weight loss, creating a vicious circle. While the core features (behavioral and psychological) of the condition are similar to those in adolescents and adults, bingeing and laxative abuse are less common among children.

It is possible that childhood AN may represent a more biological/genetic form of the disorder. Prognosis in this group is comparatively poor. Only two-thirds make a full recovery, the remainder continuing to experience difficulties. Persistent amenorrhea occurs in about 30 per cent of this group, and long-term repercussions include delayed growth, infertility and osteoporosis.

Complications of AN in Children

Physical complications include:

- *Growth impairment.* If the onset of the condition occurs before puberty, there can be permanent effects on adult stature. If the child is still ill at age 14, he or she is unlikely to be able to make good lost growth.
- *Exacerbated effects of starvation.* Children reach a more severe degree of emaciation for a similar degree of weight loss as they have smaller fat reserves than adolescents or adults.
- *Dehydration.* Children are more susceptible than adults and deteriorate rapidly when vomiting, laxative abuse or fluid refusal or restriction occur.
- *Delayed sexual maturation.* Puberty may be delayed; in girls, periods never start, and permanent damage may be done to the potential for breast growth.
- *Osteoporosis (bone thinning).* This may be more severe since

when the disorder starts before the bones are fully mineralized, normal peak bone mass is not reached.

Psychological complications include:

- *Depressive symptoms.* These are common.
- *Regressive behavior.* When distressed, children often regress behaviorally, so "tantrums" in children with AN should be viewed as an index of distress rather than naughtiness to be punished.
- *Lack of insight.* Children think more concretely than adults and are often deeply fearful. Thus they often misunderstand "treatment" as punishment for "being bad".
- *Low self-esteem and feelings of rejection.* Hospitalization may exacerbate low self-image and feelings of parental rejection or punishment, particularly if operant behavioral programs are the mainstay of the treatment.

Social/familial complications affect:

- *Family functioning.* A severely ill child creates stress for the whole family. The ill child may exert "malignant control" on the family, with rigid inflexibility, particularly around meal times. Family dynamics may perpetuate the disorder, but there is no evidence of family functioning actually causing AN.
- *Parents.* Parents may blame themselves for the disorder. Psychological problems in parents may make it harder for them to take charge of their child's eating.
- *Siblings.* Siblings suffer emotionally, feeling deprived or guilty. They may be overfed by their sibling with AN and may become embarrassed to bring friends home.
- *Schooling.* If the child becomes ill enough to be kept away from school, she misses out not only academically but also on peer group socialization. When she does attend, she may be teased and rejected by her peers. If these experiences are chronic, they may result in a deficient social network, poorly developed social skills or social phobic symptoms, thus exacerbating the child's sense of isolation.

How to Recognize if a Child Has AN

Weight loss or the failure to gain weight accompanied by food refusal may indicate a number of different conditions. The following checklist should be helpful.

- In AN, the core psychopathology, "phobic avoidance of normal body weight", is prominent.
- Food refusal, fads and fetishes are common problems in childhood, especially with young children. In most instances it is not difficult to distinguish these from AN since the characteristic preoccupation with body weight and shape is absent. Weight loss is rare and anorexic psychopathology is absent.
- A different problem is Food Avoidance Emotional Disorder (FAED). Here, weight loss is less marked and anorexic psychopathology is absent. This condition is thought to be an intermediate condition between AN and childhood emotional disorder (with no eating disorder).
- Pervasive Refusal Syndrome is a quite rare condition characterized by a profound and pervasive refusal in many areas, e.g. eating, drinking, talking, walking or self-care. While these children share some features with children with AN, their refusal characteristically spreads across other areas distinct from food or eating.
- The term "selective eating" applies to children who appear to exist on typically two or three different foods. These tend to be carbohydrate-based, such as biscuits, cereal, chips or particular kinds of sandwiches. It is quite common and there is usually no weight loss or anorexic psychopathology.
- BN, characterized by out-of-control eating behavior swinging between the extremes of food avoidance and over-eating usually followed by purging to protect against weight gain, is very rare in children, especially in those under 14. When it does occur the clinical picture is as in adults. The vomiting may or may not be admitted. If weight loss is marked, AN is primary whether or not purging occurs.
- Appetite loss may be secondary to affective disorders, e.g. depression or anxiety. Depressed individuals often suffer a lack of appetite, so children with a history of not eating need to be checked for affective disorder. As mentioned previously, the relationship between depression and AN is not clear, since

their coexistence is common and depression may be primary and causal or a secondary effect of AN.

- Appetite loss may be secondary to a medical disorder, e.g. inflammatory bowel disease, malignancy or endocrine disorder. Again, anorexic core pathology will be absent.
- Appetite loss may be secondary to some other cause, e.g. organic brain disease, psychosis, illicit drug abuse (Ecstasy, amphetamines) or prescribed drugs.

The child's school may be able to provide important information about the child's eating habits and her academic, social and emotional competence. However, if the school is involved, remember that the staff may also have little experience of AN.

The Great Ormond Street Hospital for Children operates the following diagnostic checklist to assist in identifying children with AN. A child is diagnosed with AN if he/she shows:

1 Determined food avoidance.
2 Weight loss or failure to gain weight during the period of pre-adolescent growth (10–14 years) in the absence of any physical or other mental illnesses.
3 Any two or more of the following:
   (a)   preoccupation with body weight;
   (b)   preoccupation with energy intake;
   (c)   distorted body image;
   (d)   fear of fatness;
   (e)   self-induced vomiting;
   (f)   extensive exercising;
   (g)   purging (laxative abuse).

Early Warning Signs of Anorexia Nervosa in Children

Many pre-pubescent children are now diet-conscious, often internalizing their mothers' dieting and media messages. AN can start in the absence of overt dieting (for example, after an episode of viral illness causing loss of appetite), or as a diet with a friend. How can early AN be distinguished from "normal" dieting?

- *Severity of the eating restraint.* Even early in AN, "malignant control" over eating and inability to break a diet will be evident.

44

The child with AN may become very distressed if pressed to eat what may have been a previously favourite food (e.g. ice cream). In contrast, the normal child can allow herself to be treated.

- *Denial and deception.* The child may deny experiencing hunger. She may also lie about what she has eaten, and conceal or dispose of food (for example, flushing her school lunch down the toilet or throwing her milkshake out of the window). Deceptive behavior is not a feature of normal dieting but that of an addict to starvation.
- *Hyperactivity and compulsive exercising.* Relentless activity (running rather than walking, standing rather than sitting, staying awake rather than sleeping) are characteristic features of AN. The compulsive quality and solitary nature of this activity distinguishes it as pathological. Often exercising will be denied.
- *Rate and extent of weight loss.* Weight loss is rapid and the child may try to conceal it to avoid concern. Normal prepubescent children rarely lose weight on a diet, and if they do they will proudly demonstrate their achievement.
- *Behavior around food.* A child with AN as young as age 10 may insist on preparing her own food and even that of the whole family. She may cook elaborate, high-calorie meals for others without eating them herself. Her eating may become ritualistic: she may cut her food into tiny pieces or eat very slowly. She will insist on eating less than others and may confine eating to night time or in private. Some children will vomit after eating. Such actions on the whole are not those of a normal dieter, who will try to avoid the temptation of being around food.
- *Depressed mood.* The child is likely to show signs of social withdrawal and irritability. Sleep disturbance in childhood is an indicator of depression and AN; it should arouse concern.
- *Obsessive–compulsive behavior.* Obsessive preoccupation with diet and exercise, and with rituals concerning food or exercising, are typical of AN. Other obsessions are less common but do occur.

Treatment of Children with Anorexia Nervosa

Treatment of AN is always a lot more complex than simple weight restoration, and this is especially so for children, for whom the family system has a relatively important influence.

For all children with AN – that is, all those under 18 years – the family will be involved in treatment. Formal family therapy is not necessarily the preferred choice; family counselling may do just as well. For those families that do not feel comfortable with family counselling or family therapy, parental counselling alongside individual psychotherapy for the child is just as effective and may be preferred. Whatever option is taken, it is important that the family receives support, guidance and education, since AN can have a devastating effect on family functioning.

Individual psychotherapy is a valuable adjunct to family or parental counselling in children with AN, but is not a replacement for it. There is no consensus regarding which type of individual therapy should be used; it is possible that therapist empathy, continuity and a developmental approach may be more important than the type of therapy itself. Emotional change takes longer to bring about than weight change, so long-term therapy may be needed.

Physical treatments and drug treatment may also be used. No drugs directly affect the course of the AN, but some may help with particular symptoms. If depression coexists with AN, low doses of antidepressants, taken with food, may help. If the child suffers delayed gastric emptying, a drug may be prescribed to help this.

Dietary treatment is obviously important as a major goal in the treatment of children with AN is weight restoration. This is especially important in children on the brink of puberty, as growth potential is continually being lost. If the child has reached a very low weight, a skilled refeeding programme must be implemented and the advice of a dietician should be sought; in less extreme cases a high-energy balanced diet using the portion system (see Part Two, Step 5) is advisable. Vitamin supplements are rarely necessary. Food supplements may be useful, especially in severe cases where food refusal is marked, and also if the child's weight is low but stable and the child is refusing further normal food. However, they should be used in addition to, not instead of, a normal mixed diet.

Hospitalization is likely to be necessary if the child's weight has fallen to less than 70 per cent of the normal level for age; if there are physical complications (e.g. dehydration, circulatory failure or persistent or bloody vomiting); or when there is depressed mood or other psychiatric disturbance in the child or parents.

Anorexia in Men

AN is considerably less prevalent in men than in women; men account for only about 5 per cent of cases. Apart from a few obvious sex-related differences in symptoms (e.g. amenorrhea occurs only in women), on the whole there appear to be few differences between the sexes in terms of the physical features of the disorder. Weight loss, emaciation, hormonal changes and starvation-related symptoms are found in both males and females. Men also display the characteristic fear of fatness, refusal to maintain normal weight and rigidity in thinking.

However, there are three major factors that do differentiate men and women with AN:

• Males diagnosed with AN are often obese to begin with, as opposed to females who "feel" overweight.
• Men with AN, more often than women, diet in order to attain goals in a particular sport, such as running, swimming or athletics.
• More men than women with AN began dieting to prevent themselves from developing medical conditions witnessed in other family members, such as coronary disease and diabetes.

On the whole, most men who develop AN are more obsessed than women with the exercise component. They are often compulsive exercisers, spending long hours each day jogging or doing press-ups and other exercises. While they are often as obsessed about their diet as women, they do not often show the same interest in cooking and recipes. While bingeing, vomiting and anxiety eating are as common in male AN as female AN, there is often less laxative abuse.

Certain features common in men with AN include conscientiousness and obsessionality as children: these applied to approximately a third of one group studied, while a similar proportion described dietary problems, either obesity or finicky eating habits. The presence of significant life events also appears common in the year preceding the onset of the disorder. Identifiable triggers were often related to a change in circumstances, whether through the death or departure of a loved one or a move to a new city.

Men, just like women, are strongly influenced by cultural pressure regarding appearance and roles. Over the years the pressures and expectations imposed on men by society have changed. While the traditional emphasis on strength and power is still propagated through tough, fighting, hero types in films such as *Rambo*, contemporary trends also require high levels of career success with less regard for personal relationships. Yet it is also seen as important to have a partner. Thus men are subject to conflicting demands: on the one hand to show power and strength, reflected in career and appearance, and on the other to acknowledge and express emotional needs. Internal conflict may result.

"Reverse" AN among Male Body-builders

AN has been found to be markedly more prevalent among male body-builders than among other male groups (2.8 per cent; far higher than the 0.02 per cent reported among men overall). A recent study of athletes who abuse anabolic steroids has revealed the existence of a new body image disturbance referred to as a "reverse" form of AN. The disorder, which may be associated with the abuse of the drug, is characterized by a fear of being too small, and by perceiving oneself as small and weak, even when one is actually large and muscular.

In all points except the reversal of self-perception and associated symptoms, "reverse" AN in body-builders closely resembles AN. The implication is that this body image disturbance may reflect the cultural expectations of the group, just as "normal" AN may for the young women whom it primarily affects. AN in young women has often been attributed to the increasing cultural pressures for slimness. Reverse AN may be an analogous response of young men to the influence of media pressure to be strong and muscular, as propagated through the gym subculture scene, in body-builder magazines, and in Hollywood movies.

Anorexia in the Elderly

Contrary to popular thought, AN is not restricted to the young; it can start at any time in the life cycle, including during old age. Criteria for the diagnosis of late-onset AN are the same as those for adolescent AN; self-induced starvation and a morbid fear of fatness, along with denial of the seriousness of the low body weight. Since most of these cases occur during or after the menopause, amenorrhea is not relevant. The pattern of this disorder varies greatly: in some it follows a lifelong preoccupation with weight and dieting, whereas in others there may have been no previous eating disorders.

Eating disorders are becoming more common in the elderly. Two reasons have been put forward to explain this increase. First, there has been a dramatic increase in the incidence of eating disorders in the last 30 years. Since at least 20 per cent of these disorders are chronic, and not all of those affected recover by the end of their reproductive life, some are likely to still have AN in their old age. Second, it is possible that even elderly women are beginning to succumb to the social pressures to be slim.

The diagnosis of AN in elderly patients may be more complex than in younger people, for a number of reasons. Elderly patients may be more reluctant to discuss psychological issues, eating habits or sexual issues. In some cases weight loss may have been initiated by coexisting medical or psychiatric disorders, but sustained by the individual thereafter. Weight loss may also be a symptom of one or more of the serious medical conditions that become more common during and after the forties, or be associated with major depressive symptoms, common in later years; in the latter case, there is no weight preoccupation or fear of fatness driving the weight loss. In any event, unexplained weight loss in an elderly person needs careful investigation, and eating disorders should be considered among the possible causes.

As is common with eating disorders in younger individuals, many older people with AN also have other psychiatric problems, particularly anxiety, depression and perfectionism. Overly controlled personalities are often vulnerable, especially to remembered childhood neglect or emotional distress. It seems that childhood experiences of being teased or abused remain salient and sensitive issues for some, and may manifest in an eating disorder when memories are exacerbated by a change in situation or circumstances, for example through the loss of a spouse or close friend.

There seems to be evidence that developmental milestones or phase-of-life events may serve as stressors for vulnerable women at any age, triggering AN as a maladaptive response. Younger patients report that rigorous dieting gives them an enhanced feeling of control when going through periods of loss and uncertainty. In later life, eating disorders may represent a reaction to continuing interpersonal loss – children leaving home, retirement from a job, or the death of friends or a spouse – and a similar perceived need to exercise control over some area of life.

It is important to view AN in its context. Its incidence among older women may be increasing as pressure mounts to retain physical attractiveness and sexuality. It has been suggested that some elderly women may become obsessed with thinness as a way of trying to avoid the ageing process. This particular motivation apart, the picture of AN in the elderly closely resembles that seen in younger people. Indeed, the fear of ageing and loss of sexual power and attractiveness may be as traumatic for older women as the teenage fear of not attaining the necessary perceived standards, and may be dealt with by similar psychological mechanisms (though the experience of sexual conflicts often relevant in adolescent AN does not appear pertinent in AN among elderly people).

5

What Causes Anorexia Nervosa?

AN is rarely if ever caused by any one single factor – there are nearly always several factors involved – and each individual with AN is unique. This means that there are many possible contributing causes for the condition in any one person. This chapter sets out explanations generated by different schools of thought. You may find that one or more of these applies to you, or triggers thoughts of other factors which are unique to you.

It is useful to look at the causes of AN in three categories:

- factors that make you vulnerable to developing the disorder
- factors that trigger the disorder;
- factors that maintain it once you've got it.

A single factor may act in all three ways, but it is often the case that quite separate factors are involved in the three stages.

Stage I: Factors That Make You Vulnerable to AN

It is important to understand AN can be caused by factors from within (biological or psychological), from experience or from the family environment. AN can not be accounted for by one over-arching theory, but only by an approach which considers life experiences in all areas.

While AN is distinct from other eating disorders such as BN or obesity, the themes across the three are similar: the use of food, shape and weight as a means of expressing and or controlling distress.

Figure 5.1   **Factors that contribute to the onset and maintenance of AN**

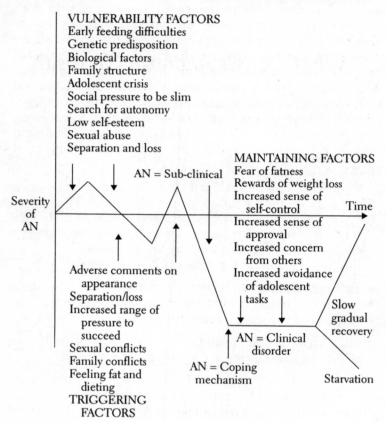

Early Feeding Difficulties

Many children develop early feeding difficulties, for a wide variety of reasons. It could be that the child is a naturally picky eater; or that the parent who is responsible for feeding, usually the mother, has a strained relationship with food herself, or has a limited knowledge of how to feed a child appropriately.

There is now good evidence to indicate that psychiatric disorders in parents have the potential to interfere with their childrearing skills and the emotional development of their children. Eating disorders are an important type of psychiatric disorder prevalent in women of childbearing age. The effect of pregnancy on a woman's body may have a lot to do with this. After all, there are few conditions which cause such rapid and radical change in body weight and shape, and this can trigger off a fear of fatness where it previously did not exist. Many young mothers experience a slump in self-esteem because of weight gain during pregnancy, and this can often be the beginning of years of dieting. Slimming magazines recount tale upon tale of women who struggled for years with their weight and date the beginning of their weight gain back to their first pregnancy. Of course, concerns about body weight may have existed long before a pregnancy.

If a mother has an eating disorder it can affect her child in a number of ways. If she is preoccupied with her own body weight to the extent that she rarely considers her own needs when it comes to eating – that is, if she eats what and when she feels she "should", rather than eating when she is hungry – this may reduce her sensitivity to her infant's needs. In short, she may have lost the ability to recognize natural feeding needs. Those who suffer from an eating disorder also frequently have difficulties in their interpersonal relationships, which can extend to the relationships that they have with their children.

In adolescence, the child can become very vulnerable to cultural ideals. Supermodels such as Kate Moss and Jodie Kidd, who are extremely thin yet considered extremely attractive, may make a teenage girl, struggling to come to terms with budding breasts and the remains of baby fat, feel overweight and ungainly by comparison. A parent who is equally unhappy with his or her own "non-ideal" body shape may reinforce the teenager's concerns. If the parent has very strong attitudes regarding shape, weight and diet, s/he may influence the child's attitude tremendously. Comments suggesting that the child is too fat or too greedy may cause great distress. Problems can also arise if the child models his or her behavior on a parent who has an eating disorder.

One of the difficulties in examining childhood eating patterns and attitudes to body weight is that this is mostly done in retrospect, when the individual has matured and already developed an eating disorder. From this perspective it is often tempting to look back and exaggerate any feeding abnormalities in childhood. Such methods of enquiry tend to lack rigour and fail to generate scientifically reliable data.

Genetic Predisposition

There is a tendency for eating disorders, like other psychiatric disorders, to cluster in families. The children of parents with an eating disorder have been found to be much more at risk of developing a similar disorder than those whose parents had a healthy attitude toward food. While the findings are nowhere near specific enough to distinguish environmental causes (i.e. learned habits) from genetic (i.e. inherited) causes, there is more to suggest that the genetic explanation is the stronger one.

Studies have shown that there is a genetic predisposition to AN and other eating disorders. One study of twins showed that if one of a pair of monozygotic (identical) twins developed AN, then the other was four to five times more likely to develop the disorder than in the case of non-identical twins. This finding, along with the evidence which shows that first-degree relatives (children/parents/siblings) of patients with AN are at an increased risk of developing the condition compared to the general population, is firm evidence that there is a strong genetic predisposition toward development of this disorder.

Biological Factors

As a species, we are very well adapted to starvation. Consider a situation such as a famine. For the famine-struck society to survive, there has to be at least a small group, particularly of women, who can cope with starvation to the extent that they survive for many months, even years, to ensure that children can be born and cared for. There must also be a group of people whose energy levels are maintained, and who respond to starvation by becoming over-active. These are the individuals who can plan and perform essential tasks despite their weakened physical state: search for food, rebuild shelters, sow and harvest crops. It also makes sense, biologically speaking, to have a group of people who become inactive and die fairly quickly, thus reducing demand on dwindling food stocks.

Starvation has a radical effect on the chemical levels in the brain, particularly levels of serotonin, which stimulates hunger and craving for particular foodstuffs and is related to the development of obsessionality. Generally speaking, serotonin is released in the brain when we start eating. The surge of serotonin, which occurs particularly with a high-carbohydrate meal, is important in producing feelings of fullness and the desire to stop eating. On the other hand, very low levels of serotonin produce hunger and sometimes restlessness. It is interesting to note that serotonin levels drop before ovulation; this may go some way toward explaining why some women have increased food cravings at this time.

Other chemical messengers stimulated by starvation come from the stomach and intestines. An important one is cholecystokinin (CCK). Low levels of CCK produce feelings of hunger and craving.

Family Structure

The stereotype of the "anorexic" family is a negative one, in which the parents are overly protective and interfering and have very high expectations of their offspring. This is a somewhat misleading model, and many differences claimed to exist between the so-called "normal" and the "anorexic" family have been shown not to apply consistently. However, there are some features of family life which do seem to relate to the development of anorexia. These are:

- A *general avoidance of conflict within the family*. This may be due to an overbearing parent or to some unspoken fear that should conflicts be acknowledged they will become uncontrollable. In such a family environment, individuals will often lose (or never develop) the ability to express and work through troublesome emotions, or confront those of others, and become unnaturally afraid of conflict even outside the family. Such people may take a pacifying role in later life, making severe compromises themselves in order to avoid conflict with others.

- *One parent tending to be over-involved with a child, while the other parent is more passive.* For example, the mother may be solely concerned with the children while the father is absent or adopts a distant attitude.
- *Family rules and sense of identity so strong that it becomes difficult for any member to express individuality.* For instance, if a family has a long tradition of producing first-rate doctors, it can be difficult for a teenager to express the wish to work in the arts, as such a wish will be seen almost as a betrayal of the family.
- *Abuse, whether of a sexual, physical or emotional nature.* Sexual abuse may take the form of incestuous relationships between parents and children, or between siblings, or the toleration of sexual abuse by a family friend or relative of a child. Physical abuse may take the form of beatings, administered by a parent or older sibling, or neglect. Emotional abuse may take the form of verbal bullying and deliberate miscommunication.
- *High-achieving parents who have similar expectations of their children.* In many cases, the child has internalized these high expectations, or may have developed them naturally. This can result in a situation where a child feels afraid of failure, and regards any effort it makes as worthless unless it is 100 per cent successful.
- *Acute sibling rivalry.* This may be created by parents and teachers who constantly compare siblings and make remarks such as, "Your sister wouldn't do a thing like that." However, this rivalry can also arise between siblings without any external forces coming to bear. For example, one 16-year-old girl felt very much in the shadow of her elder sister, and remarked that "everything she touched turned to gold", while she herself felt that she had had to work hard to achieve anything.

Things came to a climax when she entered a race, for which she had diligently trained, and her sister, who had not, won it. The 16-year-old did not consider the fact that her sister was older and stronger, but took this event as proof that she was less able. In consequence she began a diet, in order to be fitter and run faster, but within a year had developed AN.

Adolescent Crisis

Adolescence is the peak time for the onset of AN. It is in the early teens that a person develops their sense of identity and their views on the world around them. This can be a period of great uncertainty in terms of academic ability, sexuality and social skills. Severe weight loss can halt or delay development in all three areas.

The period of transition between childhood and adulthood is a very tricky one. It is an age when the desire to be older and more mature becomes very powerful, as do the seductions of adulthood (as viewed from a young perspective) such as drinking, having sex and making money. This frantic desire to take on the mantle of adulthood can result in teenagers "growing up too quickly", or behaving in ways for which they are, as yet, emotionally unsuited, such as embarking on sexual relationships at a point where they are still uncomfortable with the physical changes wrought by puberty. Alternatively, teenagers may find it enormously difficult to let childhood go, not just because they are apprehensive about the idea of being an adult, but also because those around them, particularly parents, may prefer them to remain childlike.

It is an important part of the growing-up process that young people can take "risks", such as asking someone for a date and therefore risking rejection. It is also important that they are able to do this against the backdrop of a secure home environment, where there are no risks. This risk-taking is essential as it enables the individual to establish a degree of self-reliance, to develop confidence and engage with the world in a non-fearful way. If the individual is prevented from acting independently and self-sufficiently, most commonly by over-protective parenting, their progress may be even more difficult than it would be normally.

Of course, on the part of the vast majority of parents such over-protective behavior is not malicious interference. Usually they just want the best for their child, and feel that this can only be achieved by exerting external control over their lives, perhaps in the form of pushing them academically and/or athletically. Often this is accompanied by the opinion that time spent with friends and boyfriends is wasted time, and so these activities are dismissed as trivial or actively disapproved of. Initially, a child will toe the line in order to avoid censure from or conflict with parents. However, if the child continues to behave this way, accepting parental dictates wholesale and doing the utmost to avoid conflict, feelings of pressure and entrapment can develop. The child's urge is to say "no", to make her own demands, to rebel. If she feels that she cannot articulate these feelings then she may, subconsciously, seek other ways of saying "no".

One of these ways is by refusing to eat. The put-upon adolescent comes to see her body weight as the only arena in her life over which she can exert any control. Losing weight can provide an enormous feeling of relief as it provides concrete proof of that control. It can also become a powerful statement of rejection directed at the family and home life. Losing weight can generate feelings of empowerment and superiority in an individual suffering from low self-esteem.

Social Pressure to be Slim

The Western ideal of feminine beauty has been a slender one since the 1920s. Back then, women smoked, took amphetamines and exercised in order to achieve the boyish figure that was currently in vogue. However, this mania for fashionability was pretty much restricted to the upper classes. Nowadays every level of society is aware of fashion. Magazines show us pictures of Liz Hurley in skin-tight dresses, while newspaper columns detail the extraordinarily strict dietary habits of Madonna and Claudia Schiffer. We are bombarded with images of a glamorous world that does not tolerate imperfection, particularly the avoidable imperfection of fatness. Hollywood film companies are so determined to provide images of female perfection that they often employ body doubles for nude scenes; actresses routinely have bits of their bodies airbrushed out of the final cut if they are deemed too plump. A recent American survey provided the shocking finding that, so phobic has society become about fatness, men would rather date a heroin addict than an overweight woman.

Little wonder, then, that young people growing up in this environment become obsessive about their weight and feel that, above all other aspects of themselves, this is the key to attractiveness. Magazines may very well advise on the need for adequate vitamin intake and healthy attitudes, but they will invariably accompany this sensible advice with pictures of stick-thin models in their fashion spreads. Though this may seem trivial from an adult perspective, it is necessary to remember that for an adolescent the issue of attractiveness is one of paramount importance. Therefore, the urge to be thin can outweigh all other aspirations.

For women there is an added complication. While film stars and celebrities have the legs of teenagers, they are also voluptuous. For most women, this combination is elusive. When they diet, their breasts reduce and they appear more boyish. Without recourse to surgery, they are caught between two ideals of beauty. This reflects many women's experience of life as well. They still feel caught between the need to be a successful, independent career woman and an attractive partner and loving, nurturing mother. This can be very confusing and distressing, and thus the pursuit of thinness, above everything else, can be something of a relief. Some women can convince themselves, with a helping hand from media-generated ideals, that being slim will solve all their problems, and iron out all contradictions.

The trouble is that the only problem thinness solves is the "problem" of fatness. Being slender will not make any other area of life easier. It will not make you good at your job, popular or more loved. However, lack of "results" in these other areas can often propel the person to pursue thinness all the more obsessively, long after they have achieved their original goal, as they have become so entrenched in the notion that thinness can solve everything. Many non-anorexics suffer from this belief, and throughout their lives devote time, effort and money to dieting and exercise regimes that serve only to undermine their confidence by not delivering them from their perceived state of imperfection. However, for the person vulnerable to AN this can be the point at which they become divorced from reality and see weight loss as the ultimate objective, bar none.

Search for Autonomy

When we are children we are generally content to be seen as part of a family unit and to be identified as such. When we reach adolescence, however, the great pursuit of autonomy begins. This is a natural and essential rite of passage, and for most people it goes relatively smoothly. Of course, there will be family showdowns about clothes and haircuts, suitable friends and career ambitions, but most families are able to adjust to change and give burgeoning personalities enough breathing space to grow. It is when the family is unable to adjust that problems can arise.

For instance, a family that prides itself on producing lawyers may react badly against a teenager who has determined that she will go to veterinary college. They may withdraw financial and emotional support in order to bully the child into following the family tradition. The outcome can go either of two ways. The child may react by leaving the family unit and doing her own thing, or buckle under family pressure, do as she's told and develop a sense of resentment. In the latter case, where the young student feels that she has no control over the future and her identity, she may attempt to establish her autonomy in another way. Eating is one of the classic ways of doing this, as it is so central to family life. By refusing to eat, or developing peculiar or picky habits, the youngster is demonstrating autonomy in front of the family.

This desire for autonomy does not rear its head only in adolescence. It can arise if a sibling feels herself to be in the shadow of a more "successful" brother or sister, indeed is perhaps often referred to as such. The desire to be thin may arise from a need to establish an identity that is other than that of "less successful sibling". It can also arise if a woman finds herself submerged in the role of mother and wife, and seeks to be seen as an individual rather than just an appendage of her husband and children.

However it happens, the pursuit of thinness is often based on a need to be seen as an individual, and to feel that self-will can be exercised, if only in one area of life. Thus the beleaguered adolescent who refuses to finish her lunch may be someone who is screaming to be allowed her autonomy but can find no other outlet for it.

"My father was determined that I went to his old university and studied the same subjects as he had, namely physics and maths. I didn't know how to say no to him. In fact, no one in my family knew how to do that. I did as I was told, even though I had wanted to study English literature and it was actually my best subject. The summer before I left home to begin university, we went on a family holiday to Belgium, and it was then that I began not eating. It became like a game, to see how much I could get away with not eating each mealtime. I don't remember feeling hungry or lethargic. I think the fact that I was the one in charge gave me a real buzz. When we got home and I found that I'd lost nearly three-quarters of a stone [9lbs], I felt great. It was the first time I really felt like I was doing something that I wanted to do."

Karen

Low Self-Esteem

Low self-esteem can run in families. Parents with a low opinion of themselves may pass it on to their children by comparing them unfavourably to other people's offspring. This can result in children growing up with the belief that they are not as worthy as others and having little self-confidence. Low self-esteem can develop in adolescence, when young people invariably agonize over how they match up to others and become self-critical, or when crises, such as loss of occupation or desertion by a partner, occur. Low self-esteem can be dangerous: it makes people very vulnerable, prompting them to accept relationships that may be bullying and unhealthy, or poorly paid jobs where they are put upon by others who see their lack of confidence and exploit it. It can also lead to depression, to a recurrence of illnesses and to a severely reduced enjoyment of life.

When low self-esteem is recognized as the root of your problems, there are ways to deal with it. There are excellent self-help guides (for example, the book by Melanie Fennell in this series; for details see the 'Useful Books' section on p. 183), courses and therapy sessions which can go a great way to changing individuals' perception of themselves. However, when low self-esteem is not identified as the problem, and the person continues to labour under the notion that they simply do not match up to others, the solutions sought can be unhealthy in the extreme. Alcoholism is one example. Many alcoholics turn to drink as a way of masking their negative feelings about themselves and, in a sense, escaping from themselves. AN is another. By unloading all those self-critical thoughts on to body image, a person can convince herself that, if only she lost a stone, two stones, three stones, she would become a better and happier person.

As she loses weight, she will feel a sense of achievement which will heighten her self-esteem. If the weight loss continues after the target weight has been achieved, it may be that self-esteem is now so strongly identified with weight loss that to gain weight – even if it did not rise above the original target minimum – would be severely detrimental to it. Many people with AN know that, by starving themselves, they are not tackling the real problems of their lives, but have become so dependent on extreme thinness as a way of bolstering their self-esteem that they cannot make the break from it. This is not to say that within their emaciated bodies they are bursting with confidence; quite the reverse, in fact. The problem is that, as they see it, to gain weight would make them feel even worse.

Sexual Abuse

Studies of the histories of people with eating disorders have found a much higher rate of sexual abuse than among women with no psychological problem. However, the rate of such abuse was no higher than among women with other psychological disturbances, such as depression. Sexual abuse therefore seems to be associated with psychological disturbance in general, rather than with eating disorders in particular.

There has been much debate recently as to whether women who have experienced sexual abuse or been coerced into unwanted sexual experiences are more likely to develop difficulties associated with eating. So far the results have been inconclusive.

For some women, the link between sexual abuse and eating disorders is quite clear. Some sexual abuse victims feel that they have lost control of their lives, and that the eating disorder re-establishes some form of control, however negative. Some even choose to alter their body shape to the extent that they reduce their desirability and therefore stave off further sexual approaches. Others speak of guilt, disgust and self-hatred, and use the eating disorder as a form of self-punishment. An important feature common to the women studied is that their lives had many other major problems and upheavals occurring simultaneously. Hence it is likely that the eating disorders were the result of cumulative problems rather than the single factor of abuse.

It has also been discovered that the eating disorder may have a functional purpose, that is, it is used in an attempt to solve a problem. For example, by developing an eating disorder, a person may be trying to punish the abusive parent, or the parent who failed to protect them adequately. In this instance, the changes in eating patterns and consequent eating disorder are a means of causing disruption and of attaining control. In short, the eating disorder is a stick with which to beat those who are felt to be to blame.

Certainly, for those who have suffered sexual abuse and are now experiencing eating difficulties, examining and working with their feelings relating to abuse can be helpful. A useful resource for those in this situation may be the book in this series on *Overcoming Childhood Trauma* (for details see the 'Useful Books' section on p. 183).

Dealing with Separation and Loss

Few things in life have the devastating impact of permanent loss or separation. Losing a parent, a close friend, even a beloved family pet, can turn an individual's world upside down. Death is particularly hard as most of us are without a mechanism to deal with it, especially if we have no religious faith to provide us with some form of comfort, and as those around us are suffering too. For a child it can be even worse, as a death throws up new questions of their own mortality and that of the people around them. Many children who lose one parent become morbidly obsessed with the idea that they will lose the other.

When we lose someone close to us, we experience enormous sorrow which can permeate our general consciousness for a time and lead to depression. A common feature of depression is loss of appetite, and so weight loss is fairly common in this situation. For most people, even children, this is a temporary state, and body weight will return to normal during the process of coming to terms with the loss. Even so, the journey of grief and mourning can be a long and hard one, requiring us to acknowledge our emotional needs and dependencies, and to recognize our own vulnerability. For some, the process of grieving seems an impossible task, perhaps because they feel that the pain will be too great if they give into it or perhaps because they believe that no one fully understands their feelings. They may use food as a means of numbing themselves to emotional pain. Starvation can cause this state of numbness and protect the individual by delaying the active process of grief and mourning. Because eating will restore normal feelings, they may choose to continue with the starvation. Another way of deflecting pain is by bingeing food and then purging the body of it. Eating will provide a sense of comfort and the subsequent feelings of self-loathing and desire to purge the body will occupy the mind and stave off other feelings. In this sense, BN can be seen as a way of crowding out unwanted emotions.

In recent years increasing amounts of evidence have been gathered to support the clinical observation that children and adolescents exposed to undesirable events are at a significantly increased risk of developing depression and other forms of psychopathology, including eating disorders. The most difficult kind of events to deal with are those involving the loss of someone close. This degree of crisis can also trigger adults toward depression and, in some cases, AN.

Summary

There are many reasons why a person may be prompted to lose weight and subsequently develop AN. It may be that they are influenced by external pressure to be slim, or by a desire to assert their autonomy within a restrictive family structure. They may be reacting against sexual abuse or the loss of a loved one. Whatever the reasons, it is important to remember at this stage that not all diets result in AN and not all cases of AN derive from a desire to fit into size 8 jeans.

Evidence suggests that self-esteem is one of the most critical factors in the development of the disorder. The life circumstances in which AN occurs are very varied. They may be fraught and difficult, with the vulnerable individual feeling under pressure from parents, put upon by others, or restricted in her future choices. Alternatively, these circumstances may be excellent, with supportive family, unconditional love and great prospects for the future. The common element is that the individual who develops AN, for whatever reason, experiences chronically low self-esteem.

Personality type is also an important factor. Where one personality type reacts to adolescent conflict by indulging in drug-taking or sexual activity, another personality type may exercise self-control, in the form of abstaining from food.

Finally, an inability to cope with change, be it in family structure, body shape or approaching adulthood, can make an individual very vulnerable to the development of AN, as can a similar inability in those around her.

The most important thing to be aware of is that no two cases of AN, or any other eating disorder, are exactly alike, and no one factor is at the root of the condition. It is also important to be aware of the fact that AN creates a state of mind that actually maintains the disease. We shall explore this point further in the final section of this chapter.

Stage II: Factors that Trigger AN

The second stage in the development of AN consists of the period between the establishment in a vulnerable individual of a behavioral precursor, such as dieting, through to the establishment of AN in its own right. Some of the factors described above appear to put the individual more at risk for an eating disorder by increasing the likelihood they may diet. While dieting is the common stage-setter for the disorder of AN, there are still many people who diet, successfully or unsuccessfully, without suffering from AN; the critical issue is what factors combine with a diet to result in AN. One particularly prominent element in this process, as discussed above, is low self-esteem. There is also evidence that particular kinds of adolescent conflict and difficulty, and particular personality types, tend to promote the disorder more than others.

Among the factors which have been considered to precipitate the development of the disorder are those normal to healthy adolescent development, including the onset of puberty, development of relationships (especially with the opposite sex) and leaving home, as well as more distressing events including loss of relatives, illness and others' negative comments about their appearance. Circumstances which are identified as stressful and capable of making growing up difficult are, predictably, parental psychiatric illness, parental strife, parental loss, disturbance in older siblings and major family crises. Difficulties may arise when an individual is unable to adapt well to change, or when close family or friends are similarly unable to adapt themselves well to the individual's development and maturity. These failures to adapt are usually inextricably linked, one factor enhancing the effect of another.

Stage III: Factors that Maintain AN

There are many factors which contribute to the maintenance of AN once it has become established. The behavior of the person will have changed, and so will the behavior of others close to them; therefore they will now be used to being treated differ-

Figure 5.2 **Routes into AN**

Starvation ⇨ weight loss ⇨ starvation syndrome ⇨ continuing restriction ⇨ **AN**

Starvation ⇨ weight loss ⇨ starvation syndrome ⇨ loss of control ⇨ **AN with BN**

Compulsive excessive exercise and starvation ⇨ weight loss ⇨ **extreme AN**

Binge eating and purging ⇨ BN ⇨ increased weight loss at some point ⇨ **AN**

Physical illness causes weight loss ⇨ gradual further weight loss ⇨ **AN**

ently by others. Whether or not this change in behavior of the person with AN involves adoption of the "sick" role, the individual with AN will rarely seek help. Self-starvation and the physiological consequences of under-nutrition result in a vicious circle of emotional angst and behavioral disturbance. Both the concrete behavioral pattern and emotional upset must be interrupted and addressed if recovery is to be possible.

Adolescence, as noted above, is a period of transition; it is a time for trying new behavior and gaining new experiences. Withdrawal at this time is common, be it via drug abuse, running away or phobic reactions, and AN may be considered to be such a withdrawal behavior. Once energy and effort have been invested in establishing the disorder, the individual is not going to give it up without a fight. The AN will have become so much a part of their identity and their coping strategy for difficult aspects of their life that it will be difficult for them to envisage the benefits of not having it. Some of the following elements may contribute toward maintenance of the disorder and increase difficulties regarding breaking the pattern:

1 Core features of AN itself, including "fear of fatness".
2 The rewards of weight loss, including feelings of self-control and often approval from others before any severe loss is

apparent; also avoidance of the difficult changes which occur in adolescence.

3 Body image distortion, which increases with increasing weight loss.

4 Biological effects of weight loss, which due to the starvation syndrome help to maintain the disorder, including preoccupation with food; decrease of social interest; slowing of gastric emptying, giving feelings of fatness.

6

How Can Anorexia Nervosa Be Treated?

The earlier AN is recognized and treated, the quicker and less painful the route to recovery. Delay in recognition can lead to the condition becoming more severe and therefore requiring more intensive and long-term treatment. It is a feature of the condition that individuals with AN are initially vehemently opposed to acknowledging that there is a problem and are therefore reluctant to ask for help. Thus, the average delay between onset of the disorder and its treatment is five years. Effective treatment focuses on helping the individual to take responsibility for their own eating habits, and so depends on the willingness of the person with AN to accept help. This is why forcing the issue, and strong-arming a person with AN into treatment, is unlikely to be successful.

If treatment is never sought, some individuals will develop a very severe form of AN which is resistant to all forms of treatment currently available. Such cases require prolonged and intensive treatment and care. In the one long-term follow-up study published to date, some people recovered even after 12 years of continuous symptoms; but for those who suffered for longer than 12 years, no such recovery occurred. These latter remained either chronic sufferers or died as a result of the disorder. In the light of this finding, it is clear that speed is of the essence when it comes to tackling the disorder.

Initial Steps to Recovery

- The first and most important step is for the person with AN to acknowledge that she has a problem. Though she may remain frightened of the treatment process, which requires weight gain and a challenge to her own viewpoint, recognizing that she is severely underweight and that her relationship with food is disturbed is the vital first stage.
- The second step is to acknowledge the disorder to the extent that she is willing to ask someone for help. This may be a parent or close friend, but in many cases the person with AN may be more comfortable seeking outside, professional help.
- Third, the patient must relinquish her severe dietary restrictions. This will relieve the effects of severe starvation and begin to loosen the bonds of obsession with food intake. Initially the move toward regular eating may be pitifully small, but it is a critically important change.

Specialist Treatment Services

When seeking treatment for AN, the best place to begin is with your family doctor or GP. If this is not possible, contact your nearest hospital-based general psychiatry or clinical psychology department, or a local community mental health team.

Most people with AN may be successfully treated as out-patients, using some form of counselling approach. This may be undertaken by a psychiatrist, nurse therapist or clinical psychologist: the precise designation does not matter provided the practitioner is adequately trained and experienced. Usually there will be one principal therapist who will see the patient most frequently and liaise between the GP, psychiatrist or clinical psychologist, and other health professionals. Someone seeking help with AN is likely to come into contact with a range of professionals, all with their own particular areas of expertise, working in association with one another. The following are the practitioners most likely to be involved in treating a person with AN.

General Practitioner (GP)

The GP or family doctor is usually the first professional with whom the person with AN will come into contact, either on her own initiative or through being referred by parents. In many cases, the individual will present her GP with a condition secondary to the disorder, such as depression, cessation of menstruation or constipation. The GP will take a detailed history of the condition with which she has been presented, which will lead her to diagnose the patient as suffering from AN. The stage to which the disorder has progressed will determine whether the doctor decides to refer the patient on to more specialist services or conduct the treatment herself.

In cases where the disorder is not greatly advanced, the doctor may choose to manage the patient within the practice. This may involve a nurse therapist, who can provide basic nutritional and health education, and referral of the individual to a local self-help group. This can be useful in providing information – such as resources and services which are available, including national eating disorder groups, books and dietary advice services – and assisting the acceptance and treatment of the disorder. Initial consultations will alert the person with AN to possibly unrecognized problems or conflicts in her life, encouraging her to redefine what has been troubling her. This may provide a certain degree of comfort, as some people with AN are unaware that they are suffering from a recognized condition and that their thinking is distorted. The individual will be encouraged to see her problem as a psychological one, involving a response, albeit a maladaptive one, to stress or low self-esteem, rather than as one of being in the grip of a slimming or exercise disorder. If marked improvement is not made or the condition continues to worsen, the GP will refer the patient to a specialist.

Physician

The physician may be involved in confirming the diagnosis of AN, through the administration of simple but thorough tests analysing blood and bone density. She will also undertake checks aimed at excluding other physical origins for the marked weight loss, such as diabetes or endocrine disorders.

Psychiatrist

The primary role of the psychiatrist is in the assessment and diagnosis of the patient's condition. Once this is done, she will make a decision on what form of treatment is best. The psychiatrist may choose to treat the patient herself, or refer her on to a therapist. If the psychiatrist decides it will be beneficial to prescribe drugs – as part of a comprehensive treatment approach – then she will continue to see the patient to monitor progress. Some people are strongly opposed to the idea of taking drugs as part of their treatment; they may be advised to request treatment by a therapist or clinical psychologist, who will not prescribe drugs. (For more on the use of drugs, see the section on p. 79.)

Clinical Psychologist

The clinical psychologist also assesses and diagnoses the patient, but their primary means of treatment is psychological rather than pharmacological. They may offer group or individual therapy, or a combination of both.

Psychotherapist

A psychotherapist uses long-term exploratory work, usually within a psychodynamic framework. This can involve exploring the patient's past and uncovering the initial factors contributing to the development of AN. In this form of therapy, the therapist takes an interpretative rather than a directive role, thus allowing the patient to lead the session and explore issues with which she is concerned.

Counsellor

The counsellor is there to provide psychological treatment for the patient. If the counsellor is specialized in a particular area of therapy, such as psychodynamic or cognitive behavior therapy (on the latter, see the section on p. 81 below), they will be particularly effective in that area. An unspecialized counsellor will be experienced in more than one therapy type and will be able to use that which is most suitable for the individual, possibly even using two or more kinds of therapy simultaneously.

Dietician

The dietician's role is to assess dietary intake, and to educate the person with AN on the need for a balanced and healthy diet which will provide sufficient nutrients and calories for recovery. They will also encourage the consumption of an expanded range of foods. This is particularly important as people with AN tend to subsist on an ever smaller range of foods that they deem "safe". This may come about because they have a "bad" experience with a particular foodstuff, perhaps because it makes them feel bloated and therefore "fat", or because they rule out more and more foods on account of an unacceptably high-calorie content. Expanding the food range helps to dismantle some of the fear and distrust of food.

Dieticians also encourage the use of food diaries, which they will then assess, going through them with the person under treatment. They may see the individual for a one-off treatment, or for a series of time-limited sessions. They will also liaise closely with the primary therapist, whether psychiatrist or clinical psychologist.

Pediatrician

Children as young as six have been found to be preoccupied with body shape, weight and dietary behaviors, and there have been reports of an increasing number of pre-pubescent cases of AN (see Chapter 4). Pediatricians are therefore becoming increasingly aware, when dealing with children who show signs of weight loss or poor physical development, that such symptoms may be indicative of juvenile AN.

Art Therapist

Art therapy can be especially helpful where a patient is struggling to express feelings of frustration or pain. It may be used in conjunction with other forms of treatment, or as an independent therapy. It is a welcome alternative to more traditional therapies and can be useful in illuminating important issues.

Occupational Therapist

The occupational therapist uses a variety of strategies, including projective art, relaxation, anxiety management, assertiveness training and psychodrama. A programme will be devised to suit the individual patient. For instance, body-oriented exercises may be used to correct body image disturbances, which are particularly characteristic of AN.

Principles of Comprehensive Treatment

Any soundly based programme of treatment for AN will have three core objectives:

- To increase weight so that it is within the normal range. This is the priority; only when this has been achieved can physiological functions such as temperature control and menstruation resume their normal operation.
- To help the individual re-establish normal eating patterns and to avoid extreme weight-control measure such as vomiting, laxative abuse or excessive exercising.
- To explain the physical symptoms caused by AN.

Where there is a state of malnutrition or starvation, this is treated as a priority. Starvation is known to have profound effects psychologically as well as physically, and can seriously hinder the efficacy of other types of treatment. Some form of psychological treatment is then seen as essential to confront underlying personal, interpersonal and social factors believed to foster and maintain the disorder. This may involve supportive psychotherapy, counselling about eating and dangerous purging habits and, where appropriate, other supports including relaxation, family therapy and marital therapy. The treatment programme is multidimensional, with emphasis on different forms of treatment at different stages of the disorder. One person (the primary therapist) will be the main coordinator to whom the patient can relate and through whom other health professionals liaise.

Of primary importance once weight is at a safe level is the teaching of normal eating patterns. It is important that the individual takes control of her diet as soon as possible and that, with support, she begins to manage a more normal dietary intake.

Drugs are seldom necessary but may be useful if there are complicating additional medical problems (see the section on 'Drug Treatment' below).

Hospitalization and Inpatient Treatment

Treatment as a hospital inpatient is the most intensive form of intervention which may be offered to a person with AN. Cases where hospitalization may be necessary include the following.

- Those in which weight loss has reached an extreme degree (usually defined by a body mass index below 13.5kg/m^2, see chart on p. 192). In these circumstances the sense of helplessness felt both by the person with AN and by her family can often be relieved by an intervention to break the cycle. Even so, whether hospitalization is appropriate is unlikely to depend on absolute weight alone; several other factors would usually also be considered, for example the rate of weight loss, the severity of starvation symptoms and the degree of inflexibility on the part of the person with AN.
- Those in which other disorders or associated symptoms, such as depression, self-harm, suicide attempts, obsessional symptoms, diabetes or severe purging behavior may make admission necessary to prevent the individual inflicting further severe damage on herself.

Inpatient treatment is often a lengthy process, lasting for 6–12 months; it is intensive and aims to bring about both weight gain and changes in behavior and attitude.

In hospital the individual will first be given the opportunity to take responsibility for her own weight gain, supported by the dietician and nursing team. She may exercise mildly and attend discussion groups with other AN patients to gain insight into the condition; she will also be encouraged to pursue non-food-related interests, such as art, crafts or computer skills.

If this method is unsuccessful at initiating weight gain a more structured treatment plan will be implemented. At its extreme this could involve continual observation or isolation in a single-bedded room, with bed rest until weight has risen beyond the dangerous range. Such measures are necessary at times to counter-act the extremes to which people with AN will go to avoid taking nourishment, by hiding or disposing of food, or by vomiting. The fundamental aim at this stage of treatment is to treat the person with AN until she has emerged from a critical state of health; only then is it possible to embark on less aggressive treat-ment types, such as the various kinds of therapy outlined above.

Admission to hospital has traditionally been the mainstay of treat-ment for severe AN, but is now the exception rather than the rule, since it carries a number of disadvantages. Removing the person from her everyday environment can be counterproductive and may confirm her identification with the "sick role". It also drastically reduces a person's sense of control; for someone with AN, who has fostered a sense of control for a long time through not eating, this is a severe blow, and may only strengthen the resolve to achieve fur-ther weight loss as soon as she is discharged. For these reasons, hospitalization is primarily of value to preserve life where an indi-vidual's condition has become critical and emergency refeeding and rehydration are required, followed by weight stabilization and prevention of further weight loss.

Box 6.1   Important features of successful inpatient treatment

1 Development of a trusting relationship between the patient and those there to help him/her.
2 Joint discussions regarding meals, target weights, visitors, groups, all those involved and the general ward routine.
3 Appropriate and gradual restoration of control back to the patient.

Inpatient Refeeding

There are a limited number of ways in which emaciated patients can be given the crucial nourishment they need. Intravenous feeding and tube feeding are two examples, but it is preferable if the patient can be encouraged to eat normal foods supplemented with nutritional high-calorie drinks.

Three types of inpatient refeeding programmes are discussed here: behavioral, percutaneous endoscopic gastroscopy and total parenteral hyperalimentation.

Behavioral. This involves linking weight gain or "good" eating habits with rewards, and was in the past used intensively with inpatients. It may begin with the individual confined to strict bed rest in a bare room, with gradual rewards for weight gain including increased visiting rights, movement about the ward and physical comforts, such as TV, books or radio.

This approach has not proved very beneficial in the long term; people with AN experience it as abusive and coercive, further lowering their self-esteem and increasing depression. It is, however, still used in some hospitals and is effective in some cases.

Percutaneous endoscopic gastroscopy. This is a method of supplying nutrients to the patient via a tube connected directly into the stomach, and is the form of feeding most likely to be used in very severe cases of AN. It does not affect the mobility of the patient and is used in conjunction with oral feeding. It is the more flexible form of assisted refeeding.

Total parenteral hyperalimentation. This is a means of supplying essential nutrients via peripheral or central veins. Originally used with surgical patients with gastrointestinal illnesses who could not absorb food, it has been used less extensively with AN. This treatment is useful in removing the responsibility of eating from the patient and reducing anxiety. Trials have shown the possibility of physical complications when using this technique, so it is advocated only in life-threatening cases when weight loss is extreme and unresponsive to other means of correction.

Other disadvantages of this treatment type are its long administration time, the reduced mobility it causes the patient and the distress it may cause to someone with AN who is used to total control of calorie intake and may experience a state of panic when such knowledge is removed from her.

Box 6.2   The issue of involuntary treatment

The issue of an individual with severe AN refusing treatment is rare, but on the occasions where it does happen the legal system in most countries makes it possible to admit a severely emaciated individual with AN into hospital against her will to protect against the risk of death. The individual with AN may play the system – eating to get out, resisting therapeutic measures and once away continuing in their AN as before. Therefore hospitalization is best avoided unless the patient is especially vulnerable or seeking help.

Hospital Outpatient Treatment and Refeeding

Hospital treatment as an outpatient is a more convenient and less disruptive form of help. It involves regular attendance as a day-patient for a combination of treatments that may include individual and group therapy, dietary advice, education and social activity. There is an expectation that eating is involved, at least in the form of one communal meal, and food shopping and food preparation are included. One or perhaps two meals are supervised, and participants usually attend on five days a week for as long as necessary.

The advantages of outpatient treatment are that the person with AN can gain weight at her own speed, and so can feel safe and in control. She can take responsibility for eating and, with the support and encouragement of a therapist and dietician, can relearn eating patterns and resume a normal eating regime. This maintenance of the individual's sense of autonomy is very valuable, and though weight gain is usually slow in outpatients there are pronounced behavioral and attitudinal changes which are sustained for longer periods after discharge than with inpatient treatment.

Drug Treatment

Drugs play a relatively small part in the treatment of AN, and are seldom used as the primary form of treatment. No drugs will directly affect the course of the illness, though some may be used to relieve certain symptoms: for example, antidepressants may be given to a patient also suffering from depression, just as antibiotics would be given to someone who has an infection. If drugs are used, it is as just one component of a wider treatment programme.

Drugs of the following types may be prescribed:

- *Minor tranquillizers.* These may be prescribed as a means of reducing anxiety, which is a common feature of AN, particularly around food. It used to be believed that taking these anti-anxiety drugs prior to a meal would reduce anticipatory anxiety and therefore encourage normal eating, and they were sometimes used in the initial stages of refeeding. However, concern over the addictiveness of tranquillizers has meant that they are now rarely used for such purposes, especially as they in no way address the underlying causes of the disease.

- *Anti-psychotics.* The distorted thought processes at the root of AN are at times so extreme as to be almost of a delusional nature. This prompted the use of antipsychotic medication, in the hope that it would reduce obsessionality and distortions of perception with regard to body weight. Chloropromazine was the first drug of this type to be used (sometimes in conjunction with insulin), but is now used less frequently as evidence of its efficacy is lacking.

- *Antidepressants.* These are the most commonly prescribed drugs for patients suffering from eating disorders. Their use stems from the knowledge that many people with AN suffer from depression, have had a higher than average record of depressive episodes prior to developing AN and have a family history of depression. However, although it is clear that people with AN suffer from low self-esteem, low mood and a range of depressive symptoms, it is also known that starvation can produce these symptoms, and relief from starvation can reduce them drastically. A lack of controlled drug studies and of evidence of their use in relation to AN make it difficult to assess the value of antidepressants in treatment. They are potentially helpful to those who have depressive symptoms, and it must be acknowledged that AN may be a product of a depressive illness, and that an eating disorder which has emerged in this way will serve to deepen the depression. However, even in these cases, the eating disorder requires treatment in its own right, independent of the depression.

Group Work

There are several different forms of group therapy for AN, of which the following are the main types.

Psychoeducational Therapy

This focuses on how thought processes are influenced by AN. It is a strongly education-based therapy; those who attend sessions will be taught the basic facts about what AN does to the body and what the physical and psychological symptoms are. This is not a shock therapy, and is not intended to frighten participants; rather, it presents the facts and encourages discussion and the comparing of notes.

Dietary Therapy

Carried out in conjunction with a dietician, this form of therapy concentrates on food issues, such as nutritional needs, meal planning and how to change eating patterns.

Social Skills/Assertiveness Training

Many individuals with AN suffer from a lack of assertiveness, and develop the disease almost as a means of expressing their needs. Learning to assert yourself and to interact socially can be valuable in overcoming the disorder by eliminating the need to express yourself in that way.

Peer group support helps individuals to develop a more realistic attitude in their self-appraisal, and group discussions enable them to investigate their attitudes to body weight and shape in a wider context than that to which they are accustomed, that is, within their own minds. The presence of others when undergoing therapy can be an important stage in the dismantling of the isolation that is such an insidious feature of AN.

Family Therapy

For those under 16, involvement of the family in therapy is recommended. Beyond 16 it is up to the individual whether they wish to involve family members or not. In most cases a formal family therapy programme of 6–8 weeks is unnecessary, and more relaxed family counselling is just as effective.

Family counselling involves the parents being seen as a couple, but as a separate unit from their son or daughter with AN. The main aim of this kind of therapy is to help the parents manage the symptoms and behavior of their child, and to help them overcome the sense of helplessness that they feel. Such therapy also allows the individual with AN to "come out" – to be open about their feelings and fears, with the practical support of the therapist and the emotional support of the family.

Research results are so far supportive of this type of treatment, particularly with adolescent AN. It is also proving effective with those just leaving hospital inpatient treatment programmes, and those who have failed to respond to an outpatient programme.

Cognitive Behavioral Therapy

Cognitive behavioral therapy (CBT) is a form of short-term psychotherapy. Aaron Beck, the father figure of cognitive therapy, coined the term "collaborative empiricism" to describe the nature of the therapeutic enterprise where an individual, closely assisted by a therapist, investigates the basis in reality for a personal hypothesis concerning the world. In other words, both the therapist and the person undergoing therapy examine the truths on which the latter's worldview is based. It is a very rational form of therapy, in that it guides the individual toward a realistic view of their situation by examining facts rather than feelings.

CBT is not about the therapist arguing with or haranguing the individual, or confronting them with the absurdity of their beliefs. It is about encouraging the individual to collect evidence which may support or refute their beliefs, and then re-evaluating those beliefs in the light of the hard empirical evidence.

CBT and AN: An Introduction

A central characteristic of standard cognitive behavioral therapy is its structured, time-limited framework, with each session directed by a previously planned agenda. This can suit the frame of mind typical of the person with AN, who tends to be most comfortable with order and a tight control of events. Cognitive behavioral therapy is non-historical in nature – that is, it deals purely with the present, not the past – and uses a scientific methodology. These two features often appeal to people with AN who are not prepared to delve deep into the past, perhaps because they are not yet ready to face certain deep-rooted issues, but *are* ready to deal with their disorder.

Individual and therapist work together to identify particular problem areas, for instance, the individual's belief that she is fat. In her own time, the individual embarks on a fact-finding mission regarding this area. These facts are then used to challenge the negative thought patterns that have arisen, using the cognitive skills learnt in the therapeutic sessions. An important feature of CBT is its open nature, encouraging the individual to view treatment as a series of stages without a pass/fail definition.

Mood, behavior and thoughts can all affect each other, and in the mind of the person with AN this can result in a vicious circle. A predominant belief in your own fatness can affect mood, making you feel low and panicky, which can affect behavior, making you withdraw from other people, which means that your belief in your own fatness is never challenged, thereby affecting mood and so on. The circular entanglement of mood, thought and behavior is illustrated in Figure 6.1.

Figure 6.1   **Mood, thought and behavior: the vicious circle**

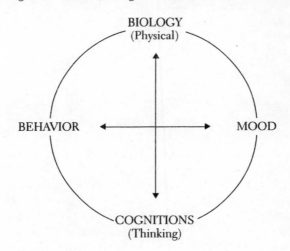

During CBT, the person is introduced to this concept as she reveals her negative, self-defeating thoughts. These are often automatic, and may rarely be held up to the light for examination. Such thoughts might include: "People are staring at me because I am so fat!" This thought would be described as a result of a preoccupation with body shape and weight. Discussion would also cover how the presence of this thought influences mood and behavior. Thinking errors would also be looked at. For instance, the belief that: "If I lose weight, all my problems will be solved" is a common thinking error in people with AN – and a dangerous one, as it allows the disease to maintain its grip. CBT is used to challenge errors such as these, which have become rooted in the mind, by seeking rational alternatives.

The self-help manual in Part Two of this book is based on the CBT model, and contains more detailed explanation of the techniques and approaches involved.

PART TWO

A Self-Help Manual

Introduction

"It occurred to me, slowly but surely, that I was missing out. I was 15 years old, I hadn't had a period in over a year, and I never went out the house except to go to school. I listened to records a lot and they sometimes made me feel very sad, because they were all about people being in love and having relationships and I was on the outside of it all. A year later, I was well on the road to recovery, my weight had reached nearly 7 stones and my skin was beginning to look healthy. I remember the morning I went to the toilet and discovered that I was having a period. I bet there can't be many 16-year-old girls who literally want to whoop because they have to wear tampons again. I felt as if I had come back to life."

Jane

If you think you have anorexia nervosa, or are some way along the road to developing the disorder, the very fact that you are reading this book is a good sign. It shows that you have recognized that you are having problems in your approach to body image and that you want to be rid of those problems. Getting from A to B is not easy, but you are probably aware of that already. The important thing at this stage is that you *want to change*.

To motivate yourself now, and as you progress, think of the reasons why you want to change. It could be simply that you feel so unhappy that you believe any state would be better than this one. However, if you allow yourself to think about your situation more closely, you will come up with more than enough positive reasons to start to change. Maybe you feel lonely and know that without AN you would feel better able to re-establish social contact. It could be that you avoid relationships with the opposite sex because you feel disgust at the thought of your own body, but wish to overcome that; or that would like to take on a new job or course of study, or pick up an old hobby again, but are prevented from doing so by the demands that AN makes on your time and energy.

Take time now to list these benefits of change, and try to create some kind of mental picture of how you would like to be. Often, being able to pinpoint exactly where you would like to end up makes it easier to get there.

Step 1

Assessing the Problem

It is important to bear in mind that you can change your attitudes to food and to your own body, but that it is not an instant process. After all, developing AN in the first place was a gradual process, not something that happened overnight.

It is also important to be aware that, if you have AN, you are likely to be very self-critical and to make unreasonable demands of yourself. When following the self-help programme that follows, bear this in mind, and consciously try not to criticize yourself when the going gets tough, or you feel that you have taken one step forward and two steps back. Congratulate yourself on every successful move forward and be easy on yourself for any slips; otherwise you may feel so hopeless that you decide to abandon the attempt altogether.

A key feature of the self-help program is the diary templates printed at intervals through the manual. Extra copies are also printed at the back of the book but you might want to photocopy these so that you have fresh pages at hand when you need them. It is also helpful to have a notebook for recording your progress as you go along, as well as for noting down your current state of mind, what you hope to achieve and what your current patterns of eating and behavior are. It is up to you whether you wish to share your written thoughts with anyone else, but it is important that you are honest with yourself, and feel uninhibited about what you write. This is, first and foremost, a record for you.

The First Steps: Where Are You Now?

To begin with you need to establish where you are now. Take

time to read through the following points, and write down your thoughts as they occur to you.

- Try to recall the things that prompted you to diet in the first place. Were you overweight, or did you diet as a means of proving yourself or asserting your individuality? For instance, did you embark on a diet because you were told not to, and you wanted to do something that showed you did not always have to do as you were told? Then ask yourself: Why was this diet so successful? For instance, did the loss of weight give you such a sense of achievement that you wanted to keep it going?
- If you feel that AN has taken a hold of you, consider the things that may be maintaining it. Try to look at your situation dispassionately, and be as truthful as you can. Your thoughts, and any notes you make, are for yourself and need not be shown to anyone else; so do not feel vulnerable acknowledging that you have developed secretive habits or deceive others in order to keep your food intake low.
- Remember that the factors which are maintaining your AN may be quite different from the ones that triggered it in the first place. It will be very helpful to consider what these initial triggers were, but be aware that understanding these is not the solution in itself.

Now try to establish what stage of AN you are at.

- You may have "pre-anorexia nervosa", which means that you have some anorexic thoughts, possibly a great fear of fatness and feelings of panic around food in situations which you cannot control, such as a family occasion. You may also have lost some weight, but do not yet have a disorder to the extent that food intake dominates your consciousness and your body weight is severely low. Refer to the Body Mass Index reckoner and the charts for boys and girls on pages 192–4, which give the means to assess your situation.
- Or you may be further along the line and have "clinical anorexia nervosa", which means that you have lost at least 15 per cent of your body weight and have been surviving on a drastically reduced food intake for over three months. At this

stage, food may dominate your daily thoughts and you may be morbidly obsessed with the idea of weight gain.

- If you have been living on a severely reduced food intake for six months, your AN has become an illness, and you may be developing some of the physical symptoms described in Chapter 2. You may feel that you are locked into anorexic behavior, that you are constantly weighing yourself, planning when and what to eat, and living an existence quite divorced from that of those around you. This is a very distressing stage of AN. You may feel very isolated and as if your view of your situation is the only accurate one.

- If your AN is more long-standing than this, the chances are that it has become a way of life for you. You may find it hard to imagine living without it, and have lost interest in everything but your AN.

If you have put yourself in either of the last two categories, take time to consider what caused you to progress through and beyond the first two stages. Was it simply the passage of time, or did the onset of depressive symptoms reduce your self-confidence and make it hard for you to reverse the process? Or did you develop rituals and obsessions that gradually expanded to dominate your life?

Keep the notes you have made, and add to them as new thoughts occur to you. You may be surprised by seeing it all written down in black and white, and the record may help you to monitor your state of mind in the future.

Most importantly, by tackling this first exercise, and thereby acknowledging that you have a problem, you have taken a giant step toward your recovery.

Should You Seek Professional Help?

It is a sensible precaution to seek professional help if you have AN, if only to ensure as you embark on the self-help program that your restricted food intake has not triggered any further medical complications. However, there are some situations in which it is particularly advisable that you consult professional medical practitioners.

- If your AN is of a bulimic nature, it is wise to have your heart and blood pressure checked regularly.
- It is particularly important for women who have ceased to menstruate as a result of AN to seek medical advice. (In most cases menstruation will resume upon the return to a normal body weight.)
- You should also seek professional help if you are suffering from severe depression, either independent of or as a result of AN. The reason for this is that depressive illness may hinder any attempts on your part to improve your situation on your own, as it may rob you of the necessary motivation and self-belief that a self-help program requires. In such cases, a doctor may prescribe antidepressants to alleviate some of the depressive symptoms.
- You may wish to seek external help if you feel that you need support to make change, and have no one in the family or close environment who can fulfil that role. In such cases a therapist, GP or support group may be able to help.
- Finally, if you find that, upon reading through the following steps in the program, you instinctively react against the changes suggested, and find that you cannot counteract this instinct, do seek help.

Awareness of Obstacles

It is only realistic to acknowledge that changing your behavior and attitudes is not going to be easy. Reviewing the likely obstacles to change does not mean taking a negative or defeatist attitude: on the contrary, if you take a clear-sighted look at the ways in which resistance to change might affect you, you will be better prepared to deal with them if and when they arise, rather than taking them as reasons to give up.

Lack of Commitment

If this self-help program is to work, you must make a commitment to change. Initially this will seem alarming – even like stepping off a cliff into space – but in fact you are not stepping into the unknown. You have been free from AN before, and there is no reason why you cannot be again.

Be aware of any tendency to procrastinate, and try to stop yourself from reasoning yourself out of making the change now. There will be no time that seems exactly right, so commit yourself to beginning, and stick with that commitment. Keeping a diary, as described below, can help to reinforce commitment; in the following steps of the programme you will learn techniques to counteract your wavering, and be able to record your use of them and build on them.

Fear of Losing Control

The chances are that your life is completely organized around your AN. In a sense, although you may feel that AN gives you a way of exercising control, it is your AN that has taken over the reins and is controlling you. What you are seeking to do now is to regain genuine control for yourself – even though at times it may not seem that way as you will be faced with challenges that are difficult to overcome, and will have to break your previous strict patterns of rigorous self-control. Try to keep to the forefront of your mind the essential fact that you are not relinquishing control, but restoring it to yourself. Currently, it is not you who are in control – your AN is.

Fear of Change

All major life changes can be terrifying – even the positive ones, such as having a child or getting a promotion at work – and yet without change, our lives stultify. For people with AN the fear of change is especially strong because they cannot conceive that it will make them anything other than more unhappy than they are currently. Challenge this thought as it occurs. Even when it is hard to believe, the truth is that you will be happier once you have made, and accepted, these changes. Following this program and combating your AN is one of the most positive and rewarding changes you will ever make in your life.

Isolation

AN works in a very insidious way, and isolates the person suffering from it. If your AN is reasonably advanced, you may already have withdrawn from social relationships and feel that you have become separated even from close friends and family. However, you are less alone than you think. Those around you may seem distant, but much of this is to do with the fact that they do not know how to approach you, and are frustrated by their seeming inability to help. If you crave support, ask for it. If it is not available close at hand, then seek it from professional services or from an eating disorder support group. Not only will this take you out of your isolation, you will find that you are not the only person in the world to be dominated by anorexic thoughts, and not the only person seeking to be free from them.

Self-defeating Mechanisms

Be aware of the fact that your AN is not going to give up without a fight. You have probably already developed a complex system of thought that is hard to break free from, and one aspect of this is a tendency to tell yourself you are not capable of change. Avoid interpreting every setback as proof that you cannot achieve change. Think of the example of a smoker, who quits entirely for three months and then, one night at a party, smokes five cigarettes. Is that single occasion proof that the person is incapable of quitting and should therefore just give in and return to smoking regularly? Of course it is not, and most would-be ex-smokers will recognize this. Learn to concentrate on your successes and count them as proof of your ability to change. Self-defeating mechanisms can themselves be defeated; all you need to do is recognize them for what they are.

Developing Motivation for Change:
The Pros and Cons of Anorexia Nervosa

It is important to remember that AN may have helped to solve many of your problems. You didn't develop AN because you are crazy, neurotic or self indulgent. You developed it because it was a solution to many of your problems or feelings that were present before the AN started. Looking at the advantages of having AN symptoms may help you understand why the disorder developed and why it is so hard to consider giving it up.

Make a detailed list of all the advantages of having AN. Don't be defensive about this. Remember that developing AN was an adaptive solution to your problems at the time. Always start with the advantages first. Then make a list of all the disadvantages. It is likely that at this stage the pros will outweigh the cons. If this is the case don't panic. It merely emphasizes that AN was an adaptive and understandable solution for you. If you find it difficult to do this exercise enrol the help of a trusted friend or relative. Ask them what they see as the advantages and disadvantages for you. Again, urge them to be open and honest. Encourage them to put points in both columns. Listed on p. 96 are some typical advantages and disadvantages that AN sufferers often report.

What to Do with the Pros and Cons List

First, simply making the list may help you look differently at your current situation. Maybe writing down all the disadvantages will help you realize how hard it is to maintain the AN. The list will give you lots of experiments you can do using the cognitive techniques described later in this book. Take each statement in turn and look at it in detail. Re-phrase each statement as a question, for example, "Does starvation really improve my mood"? and then test it out over a few days keeping note of what evidence you find.

Projecting into the Future

Perhaps it is the case that the advantages clearly outweigh the disadvantages just now. Try imagining what it would be like in one year, two years, five years or ten years' time. A good way of doing this is to imagine a meeting with a close friend who doesn't have AN. At each meeting, imagine that you are the

The pros and cons of AN

Advantages	Disadvantages of AN
1. I feel in control of myself and my body this way.	1. Although I don't eat, I think about food all the time. It's exhausting.
2. No one can think I am indulgent or greedy when I look this way.	2. I have cravings about food which are hard to control.
3. People take more notice of me, I get compliments and attention.	3. I am terrified that I might binge.
4. I can wear clothes that I never dreamt I would be able to wear.	4. I am cold all the time, even in the summer.
5. Things in my family have changed. They show me concern rather than ignore me now.	5. At times I feel exhausted and weak.
6. When I starve, my mood improves.	6. I am missing out on my old social life because I cannot eat with others.
7. My self-esteem is better.	7. I am more irritable.
8. I have much more confidence.	8. My sleep is disturbed.
9. My body no longer feels disgusting.	9. My concentration gets bad, particularly at the end of the day.
10. I feel pure and clean.	10. My skin is dry and itchy.
11. My sex drive has disappeared.	11. I worry about my fertility.
12. I can concentrate on work and don't have to bother with food.	12. I worry about my bones.
13. The thinness protects me from close relationships.	13. I have become even more preoccupied about my body and shape.
14. If I have AN I get psychotherapy.	14. I feel guilty about being this way, it is self indulgent.
15. I can run easily, I don't have to train any more.	15. I cause my family a great deal of worry and stress.
16. My periods have stopped.	16. I have to keep going to the doctor.
17. Men pay me less attention. If they do show interest it is concern.	17. I am terrified I may end up in hospital.
18. I feel independent and free this way.	18. It is such an effort, can I keep going this way?
	19. My mood crashes for no reason.

same, and that you have to say what you've been doing and what has been happening in your life since the last meeting. Then turn things around and imagine what he or she might say. If you cannot do this on your own, try it for real, with a close friend. Some times it is only when you can look five or ten years ahead and see how much of life you may have missed out on because of the AN that it will really come home to you that you do need to change. For example, in ten years' time you might still be saying "Well, I've still got anorexia nervosa; I'm still very thin; I'm still in control; it is still a battle every day; I haven't formed any new close relationships; I never completed college. My life revolves around food and dieting." In contrast, your friend might be saying that she has a new job and is about to get married; that she is moving to a different part of the country; she has developed a new circle of friends; and that she had a really good trip around Europe last summer with her fiancé.

Writing a Letter to your Anorexia Nervosa

If you do finally decide to change, giving up AN will not be easy. You may go through a period of grief or a sense of loss, as the AN may have served you well over a number of years. One way of coping with this is to write a letter to your AN as though it were a friend you were saying goodbye to and will never see again. Write about all the good times you have had together, what you will miss, and how you will cope without it. This exercise might help you distance yourself from your AN and come to regard it as something that is separate from you, rather than an integral part of you.

It might also be useful when you have written the letter to do something symbolic with it, such as put it in an envelope and seal it up and put it away, or to burn it. Sometimes keeping the letter and re-reading it may be helpful. Following is an example of a letter written by a patient of mine who eventually decided to change after 10 years of severe AN.

Dear Anorexia Nervosa

I am sorry that we have to part. You have been my best, most loyal and most trusted friend for the past ten years. You have never let me down, always been there for me, and I could always turn to you when I was most distressed.

No one else has stood by me like you, day in day out, year after.

I don't know how I will cope without you, but I am determined to try. I feel very frightened about not being able to turn to you in future.

I also feel angry with you. I thought that I could control you, but gradually you came to control me. You never left me alone, even when I thought I was coping without you, you tormented me and tricked me back into your grasp. At times I really hate you for what you have done to my life. Maybe I will cope without you. I am certainly going to try. I want you out of my life. I want you separate from me, I want peace from you, leave me alone.

I'll miss you.

Love, Anna

Coping with Your Family

In many cases, this section might be better entitled "The Family's Guide to Coping with You". The following paragraphs are written under the assumption that you live at home, though the suggestions made can easily be adapted to help you cope with your family (and them with you), no matter what your family circumstances are. The idea is to encourage you to do some preparatory work, including considering a number of questions about your close relationships, before you move on to the next step of the program. In this way you can start to change your environment in such a way as to support you better as you set about making changes in your behavior and attitudes.

- First of all, read again the section entitled "Family Structure" in Chapter 5.

- Next, read through and answer the questions below ("Assessing the Relationship of your AN to your Family"). Note that these questions do not have correct or incorrect answers; they are designed to start you thinking about your AN in the context of your home and family life.
- Finally, work out a plan, either alone or with your family, to cover the areas you wish to tackle.

Assessing the Relationship of your Anorexia Nervosa to your Family

Consider what would change for the positive within your family, if your AN disappeared this instant.

- Would familial tension be reduced? That is, would there be fewer arguments or potential arguments?
- Would you be able to eat meals together like a normal family?
- Would your parents/siblings/partner/children be less anxious about you? Or less frustrated with you?
- Would you be able to enjoy activities as a family?
- Would you be closer, as a family? Would you individually be closer to any family members?
- Are there any other changes which would be positive?

Now consider what negative changes might occur if your AN did not exist. If you cannot think of any, cast your mind back to the first few weeks and months of your AN and try to remember the differences between then and now.

- Did your family/members of your family show more interest in you? And would that interest diminish if your AN disappeared?
- Did you get to have things your own way? And would you return to not having things your own way?
- Did you/do you enjoy playing the "sick role", and being regarded as incapable of doing certain things and in need of extra care? Would the relinquishing of that role distress you?
- Are there any other changes which would be negative?

Formulating a Plan of Action

The actual process of formulating a plan can be of enormous

benefit, particularly for family members who feel frustrated and helpless in the face of AN. It is important to be assertive when formulating this plan; allowing yourself to be bamboozled into doing what others want may only exacerbate your condition by increasing the desire to assert control over your life through food.

Use your answers from the assessment above to help you. For instance, if you feel that one of the positive aspects of not having AN would be being able to have normal meals with your family, then this should be written down as an aim. Discuss this issue with your family, and set yourself a target of, perhaps, sitting down with them to one meal per week. At first you may be unable to eat exactly as your family do, but keep in mind that that is what you are working towards. Perhaps they could meet you halfway, by eating a meal which you could comfortably share.

Though it may seem a little scary at first, it can be a tremendous relief to engage with your family in this way, and to allow them to help you loosen your self-control – and your isolation.

If you found that one of the negative aspects of being free from AN was that you would receive less attention from your family, then request the time to discuss this with them. Do other family members feel this way? Is yours a family in which only negative behavior and events get attention, while good things are ignored? If so, try to think of ways in which the focus can be turned toward the positive. Instead of emphasizing where problems lie, and devoting energy to lamenting situations, try emphasizing the good aspects of situations, focusing on achievements and successes.

When implementing a plan of action, try to approach it in a reasonably businesslike way. Take it seriously, and take note of its progress. It is unlikely to go 100 per cent smoothly, and you may suffer setbacks, but don't let this put you back at square one. The very fact that you are involving your family is a step forward, and you may make unexpected leaps and bounds as they become more involved.

Anorexia as a Weapon

Some people with AN use the disorder as a stick with which to beat their family, It may be that the family focuses on the negative, as described above, and that the individual with AN feels that she has been consistently ignored in favour of siblings/relatives/parents who are ill/in trouble/in distress. In some cases this can result in a sibling developing AN in response to another family member's AN.

Alternatively, someone may feel that she is expected to conform to a family pattern, such as high academic achievement, and develop the illness as a way of declaring her individuality and rebelling against constraining expectations.

If you feel that your AN is in some way a weapon, it is important to establish, even if only in your own mind, why this is so. If you want to broach the issue with your family but feel that they won't listen to you, or simply that you don't know how to begin talking to them about such issues, then family therapy may help. A family therapist can act as an intermediary, helping you and your family to articulate how you feel and assisting in negotiation.

As in relation to obstacles generally, awareness of the factors affecting your family relationships is extremely important, and can be a vital first step in tackling AN. The next stage is to act on it rather than hide behind your AN. However angry or impotent you feel, be aware that holding on to your AN, though it can be a powerful weapon and can produce the responses you want, is only a temporary expedient. You are only treading water emotionally if you stop here.

Anorexia and Other Relationships

Anorexia can be enormously destructive to relationships outside as well as within the family, whether with friends or partners. AN can halt any kind of natural development in partnerships, and make the partner feel very hopeless and isolated. Many people with AN find that, due to a chronically poor self-image, they become reluctant to have sex, and may terminate the physical side of the relationship altogether. Naturally this can be devastating for the partner, who feels rejected.

The most destructive effect of AN on a relationship is that the partner may feel responsible, and is almost certain to feel in the dark. This can result in showdowns about eating and weight, which have little effect other than to put further strain on the relationship.

The first step here is to enlighten your partner, as far as you are able. Explaining how you feel and why you are driven to restrict food intake to such an extent will ease some of the strain; setting ground rules, such as requesting that your eating patterns are not interfered with, can go some way to re-establishing links. If your partner feels uncomfortable discussing your AN, which can happen if they are fearful or reluctant to acknowledge the existence of the disorder, then a therapist who can talk to you both may be helpful.

When you are ready to make changes, enlist your partner's support. Not surprisingly, they are usually more than happy to help. The important thing is to make it clear at what rate you intend to make these changes, and that you should not be criticized when you lapse. Above all, keep open the lines of dialogue.

"We had reached a stalemate. My husband asking for sex, and my avoiding it. Occasionally this would erupt into a confrontation, and I could see that he felt hurt and rejected, but he couldn't see that, as I lost more and more weight, I felt increasingly disgusted with my body and found the thought of intimacy unbearable. I did try to explain how I felt but he didn't want to hear it. He would listen in stony silence and say nothing. I began to realize that he was frightened of the idea that I wasn't 'normal'.

"When I asked my GP to refer me to a therapy group, I told my husband, but he seemed uninterested. He would drive me to the group, wait outside for me, and drive me home, all the time saying nothing.

"After a few weeks, he wanted to know why I wasn't getting better!

"The breakthrough, such as it was, came in fits and starts. I was learning assertiveness techniques, and how to articulate what was happening with me, through talking to other people with AN. It began with me making long, rambling speeches and him listening, silently. Finally I asked him to help me by

reading through my plan of action. I wanted to stop thinking along anorexic lines, and to do so meant that I had to face the fact that weight gain was necessary. I told him that I found the idea frightening, and that I needed someone to reassure me. He promised to help me. Though he found it awkward, and would refer to the difficulties I was having as 'the problem', we did start to feel more at ease with each other, and my AN stopped being something that kept us at arm's length and began almost to be something that made us closer."

Angela

Step 2

Monitoring Your Eating

- The next step after assessing the problem is to monitor your current eating patterns. It is important to do this before attempting to make any changes.
- Recovery from AN involves you learning to relax over eating and reprioritizing your life so that food takes a less prominent position.
- Recovery from AN involves *risk-taking* and *challenging* your previous patterns of eating.
- Change may seem daunting, even terrifying; but if you feel intimidated by the prospect, try to remember how miserable you were feeling when you initially asked for help.

Keeping a Food Diary

The first concrete step is to record daily everything that you eat and drink. You may find it helpful to use the diary sheets provided here (and at the end of the book). If you have access to a photocopier, copy the blank sheets printed here and keep them together when you have filled them in. If you do not, buy a notebook and make a diary yourself, following a similar layout. It will help if your notebook is of a small, convenient size so that you can carry it with you at all times.

You will see that the diary sheets have four columns to the right of the spaces where you will record what you eat and drink. The first column, headed "Por", is where you will record the number of portions you have eaten when you use the portion system outlined in step 5; don't worry about this for now. You

Monitoring Your Eating

Diary 1

Date: _____   Day: _____

	Por	Vom	Lax	Ex
Breakfast				
Snack				
Lunch				
Snack				
Evening Meal				
Snack				
Totals				

can and should, however, record from the beginning in the appropriate columns when and how many times you vomit ("Vom"), take laxatives ("Lax") and/or exercise ("Ex") after eating. You should also record in the wide left-hand column any binges you may have and what you consumed in them; these foods and drinks should be placed in brackets.

Try to keep your food diary up to date through the day rather than waiting until the evening to remember what you have eaten throughout the day. If you write down everything as soon as possible after eating and drinking, it will be easier to make sure the record is accurate.

People take differently to diary writing. Some find it helps them feel in control and easily maintain a full, accurate diary, while others find it hard and time-consuming. If you find it difficult, try to focus your efforts on particular days: two fully recorded days out of a week will be more valuable than a whole week of semi-completed days.

You may well find at first that your diary shows a very self-restrained diet, with lots of black coffee and diet drinks and very definite patterns of "allowed" foods. You may also notice how you use exercise after eating to "work off" the meal. The next step is to try to make yourself more aware of, and to move toward, the principles of normal eating.

Principles of Normal Eating

The principles of normal eating, shown below, are a set of *targets* toward which you should aim – not a set of *rules* which must all be kept rigidly all at once. Your plan is to take *steps* toward normal controlled eating, testing out each new practice at a pace that is tolerable to you, even if this means that progress appears to be very slow. Remember, you are more likely to lose heart and give up if you try to be too ambitious too soon than if you persevere little by little and give yourself time to get used to different ways of eating.

Once you have managed to follow these guidelines for some time, you will then be in a much stronger position to make more substantial changes to your diet and eating patterns.

- Eat in company, not alone.
- Do not do anything else while you eat (except socializing), even if you are bingeing. For instance, do not watch TV or read. You can listen to music, especially if this helps you relax, but the important thing is that you should try to concentrate on enjoying your meal.
- Establish a regular eating pattern. Plan to eat three meals a day plus three snacks, at pre-determined times, in the sequence: breakfast; snack; lunch; snack; dinner; snack. Plan your meals in detail so that you know exactly what and when you will be eating. The idea is that you should try to keep one step ahead of the problem.

It cannot be stressed too much that these principles are recommendations to aim for; you are highly unlikely to achieve them quickly or without taking risks and experimenting. The important thing is that you become aware of a different, healthier way of fitting food into your life.

Helpful Tactics

There are various ways in which you can help yourself as you set out on your journey towards change. The task ahead of you is a hard one, so do take every opportunity to make it a little easier.

- Try to think of an activity you may enjoy doing that does not involve food (avoid cooking) or intense calorie-burning (avoid aerobic exercises or sport.) Examples could include drawing, painting, reading, learning a new language, pottery, visiting the cinema. It could be some activity you used to enjoy but have not participated in for years. Make time to do this.
- Identify triggers which are most likely to cause you to restrict food intake, using your recent experience and the evidence provided by your diary. Examples could include comments about your weight or eating habits, or a friend or relative starting a diet and eating less. Think through these situations

and write them down, along with reasons why you think they should not affect you. Then you can refer to these later should any of the situations arise and tempt you to cut back on your eating.

- In whatever ways possible, avoid obsessing about food and weight. If you have spent time poring over recipes and cookbooks, or have been cooking for the family, try to wean yourself off these activities and fill your time differently (this will be easier if you have identified other activities, as suggested in the first point in this list).

- Try hard not to weigh yourself more than once a week. If possible, stop weighing yourself altogether.

- If you suffer from the anxiety and depression that commonly accompany AN, remember that they will become less severe as you gain weight. However, if you can identify particular problems which are clearly getting you down, focus on them and try to do something positive toward solving or at least minimizing them.

- If you are exercising, ask yourself what you get from it: if it is merely to burn calories, try to think of a sport or activity that is more fulfilling and will give you more genuine satisfaction for its own sake.

- Do not worry if you have not had a period for some time, or indeed ever. When your body returns to a healthier weight your periods will also return, symbolizing the return of your whole body to normal functioning.

- The occasional drink of alcohol may be beneficial in helping you to relax and cope with eating a fuller diet. Taken now and then, and in moderation, it may help ease you out of the pattern of restricting.

- Set aside some time daily to reflect on how you are coping. If some of your strategies are not working, try others.

- Set yourself limited, realistic goals; work from hour to hour rather than from day to day. One failure does not mean that a succession of failures will follow.

- Note your successes, however modest, in your diaries. Every time you eat normally you are reinforcing your new good eating habits.

Summary

- In order to begin to change, it is important to record your current eating and drinking patterns. A daily food diary is a good way to do this.
- It is also important to begin to become aware of, and to try to work toward, the principles of normal eating.
- There are various ways in which you can make life easier for yourself as you embark on the self-help program.

Homework assignment for Step 2

- Use a food diary to monitor your eating patterns. You could use the diary sheet provided here, or make up your own in a notebook.
- Try to work on at least one of the "principles of normal eating" each week. Write it down in your notebook.
- At the end of each week, review your food diary and note any changes, positive or negative, in your eating patterns. Spend some time thinking about how these were brought about and whether you found them hard or easy to make.
- Try to put into practice some of the tactics suggested to make it easier for you to begin to change.
- If you find you are unable to keep up a diary, or to make any progress at all towards principles of normal eating, don't worry; just go back to the beginning and try again. Remember, you wouldn't expect miracles from other people; so don't expect them of yourself.
- Don't forget to reward yourself for any achievements you have made, no matter how small.

Step 3

Challenging the Way You Think, I: Automatic Thoughts

How Thinking Affects Behavior

The diagram below shows how thoughts, behavior and mood are inter-related, and how a vicious circle can arise as a result.

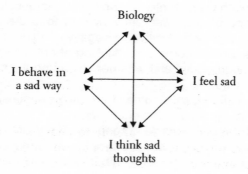

For instance, imagine for example you caught a cold. The physical effects that this has on you (biology) make you *feel* weak and apathetic. This in turn may make you *think* more negatively, e.g. "I look so awful today – all pale and puffy faced. I'd better stay in." The result of thinking this in turn affects your *behavior* in that you stay inside longer. By staying in, you may get bored and start to feel more negative about yourself – and thus the cycle is perpetuated.

In the same way, a vicious circle is set up in AN. The effect of thinking about fat and how you ought to be thinner has a direct effect on your behavior, prompting you to diet, starve, exercise, vomit, etc. These behaviors lead to restricting food intake and therefore trigger more thoughts about food and eating. This restrictive eating pattern also has a direct effect on your biology – it causes lack of concentration, sleep disturbance, irregular periods and so on – and often results in you feeling low in mood.

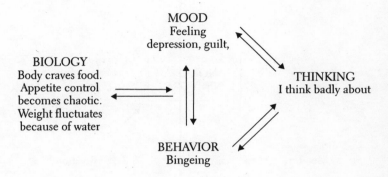

Can you think of any examples of vicious cycles like this affecting you? Write down some examples using the model contained in the diagram to make links between biology, behavior, thinking and mood.

There is little you can do directly to change your mood, although some medications may help by working on the biological symptoms of depression. What you can do is learn to think less negatively about yourself, about food and about your weight. This will enable you to change your behavior, introducing the principles of normal eating, and thus to break out of the cycle. Cognitive behavioral therapy provides a way of doing this.

AN and Distortions in Thought

AN is an eating disorder which affects your mood and the way you think, feel, behave and interact in relationships. Even when the behavioral symptoms of AN have disappeared and you are eating normally, the anorexic thoughts or preoccupations with food, weight and eating often remain.

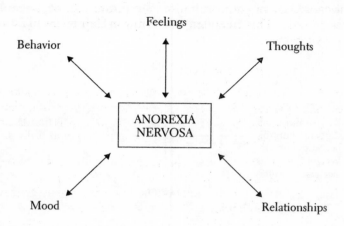

Typical anorexic thoughts include:

- People are staring at me because I'm so fat and gross.
- Everything will be all right when I lose some more weight.
- I must always exercise after eating to stop the calories turning to fat.

These thoughts, while they seem to make sense on the surface, are distorted and are not helpful to you, because the issues around which they revolve may have come to preoccupy most if not all your thoughts, so that you are unable to apply yourself properly to anything else; in other words, they have come to dictate how you lead your life. These thoughts also impede progress because they represent arguments that encourage you to maintain your faulty eating pattern.

Typically, someone with AN believes that she is the only person in the world who thinks and behaves as she does, but when she talks to others with AN is amazed to find that there are many in exactly the same position as herself.

Cognitive distortions – distortions in the way you think – don't just affect you. If you think in this way, you will have a negative view not only of yourself, but of the future and of the world around you. (This triad can also occur in depression, BN and severe anxiety.)

What CBT Can Do to Help

Cognitive behavioral therapy is aimed at helping you *learn to recognize errors in your thinking which prevent you from changing your behavior.* By using this manual, which is based on a cognitive behavioral approach, you will:

- learn to apply your reasoning skills to situations you find difficult, in particular those related to your eating;
- learn to find alternative ways of thinking that will help you to change your behavior and make you feel better;
- be encouraged to think of yourself as a scientist, testing out or experimenting with your ideas to find out how realistic or helpful they are, by choosing practical tests to undertake at each stage of the programme.

Understanding Automatic Thoughts

Having automatic thoughts is normal. Everyone has them, and they can be "good", "bad" or "indifferent". We will all have thoughts running through our minds the whole time, although we are not always conscious of what we are actually thinking. Nor do we normally question our own thinking; therefore, even if it becomes excessively negative or self-critical, we tend just to believe that the thoughts are factual. However, how one thinks about oneself can be very strongly affected by all sorts of factors such as life circumstances, self-confidence, body image, etc.

If you have AN, you probably have powerful automatic thoughts that come into play to prompt you to starve or exercise excessively. In this step you will learn to recognize and counter your own "automatic thoughts"; but first you must be quite sure of what an automatic thought is.

Characteristics of Automatic Thoughts

- They are automatic: they are not actually arrived at on the basis of reason or logic, but just seem to happen. It can help to think of them as part of the running commentary on life that goes on inside our heads almost constantly while we are awake.

- They are our own interpretations of what is going on around us, rather than facts. They depend on all sorts of factors, such as our level of self-confidence and how things are going in our lives generally. If we feel confident and happy, then the automatic thoughts we have are likely to reflect this by being positive and optimistic; however, if we feel unhappy and low in confidence, the automatic thoughts are likely to be negative and pessimistic.

- Negative automatic thoughts are often unreasonable and serve no useful purpose. They are based on an individual's view of herself, and often do not coincide with reality. Even if they are not actually irrational they make you feel worse. They can prevent you from getting better by persuading you that there is no point in trying to change, even before you have tried to do so. They may allow you to justify putting things off. "There is no point in my working through this manual, I'll be wasting my time; I've had AN for such a long time, I must be a hopeless case."

- Even though these thoughts may be unreasonable and/or unhelpful to you, they probably seem very believable at the time when you actually think them, and because they are automatic it is very unlikely that you stand back from them and evaluate or question them. You tend to accept them as easily as an ordinary automatic thought such as "I should answer the door" when the doorbell rings.

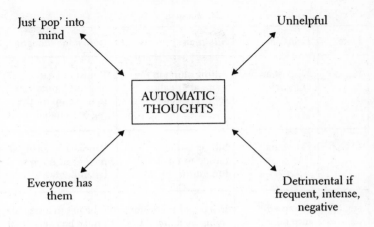

Recording Negative Automatic Thoughts

The next step is to record your negative thoughts in your diary. If you start to feel bad for any reason, review your thoughts. Try to catch exactly what has just passed through your mind. These are the thoughts to write down; they can be seen as your automatic reactions, either to something that has just happened or to an issue which you have been thinking about, such as your AN. You will probably find that these thoughts are very negative and that you believe them.

It is important to try to recognize some negative thoughts of your own. Below is an excerpt from the cognitive therapy diary of a 21-year-old student who had suffered from AN for four years. This may help you to identify some of your own negative automatic thoughts. If so, jot some of them down in the blank diary page provided (or on the larger, blank versions provided at the back of the book). *Don't worry* if none comes to mind immediately. You will have a chance over the next week to add some to your food diary.

The typical automatic thoughts of a person suffering from an eating disorder tend to be preoccupied with food, weight and shape. Some further examples are:

Diary 2

Date	Emotions	Situation	Automatic thoughts
12.5.96	Disgust/anger at myself	Sitting alone in my room after eating some chocolate	I must not eat anything tomorrow to make up for the pig out I had tonight
14.5.96	Fear/panic	Sitting in the dining room at lunchtime	People are staring at me because I'm so fat and ugly
15.5.96	Ashamed, miserable	In a department store trying on a dress	If I can't fit a size 10 I must be overweight

I look so fat in this dress, I may as well go home |

Diary 2

Date	Emotions	Situation	Automatic thoughts

- If I lose a stone, my life will be OK.
- I feel ashamed of my figure. If I was slim people would like me more.
- I'm no use – I'm so fat and ugly, I have no control of my life. When she said "You look well" she meant "You look fat."
- It's not worth living if I get any fatter than this.
- I'll never be the person I want to be.

Summary

- Anorexia nervosa affects not just the way you behave but also the way you *think*.
- Preoccupations with food, weight and eating often remain even once the behavioral symptoms of AN disappear; these need tackling to prevent faulty eating patterns from reappearing.
- There is a close interrelationship between *thoughts*, *mood* and *behavior*. If one becomes disturbed a vicious negative circle can then ensue.
- *Automatic thoughts* are those that just pop into the mind without being consciously formulated. Everyone has them but they become detrimental when they are repeatedly of a *negative* nature.
- Cognitive therapy involves recognizing and altering negative automatic thoughts.

Homework assignment for Step 3

- Continue completing your food diary as outlined in Step 2.
- Remember to continue trying to work toward the "principles of normal eating".
- Using the diaries set out here, try to write down some negative automatic thoughts during the coming week.

(continued on next page)

Put the date in the first column and fill in the other three columns headed "Emotions", "Situation" and "Automatic thoughts", describing how you felt, what the situation was at the time, and what thoughts came into your head.

- If you find it difficult to identify your automatic thoughts, don't worry; it is a difficult technique to master. Imagine yourself in some situations and think how you would react in each one. For example, ask yourself: What went through your mind when you first looked at this self-help manual? What do you think when you look in the mirror? (Or, if you avoid doing this, what thoughts stop you from doing so?) What goes through your mind when you first meet a new group of people? This may get you in the swing of catching the thoughts that just pop into your mind.

Step 4

Challenging the Way You Think, II: Thinking Errors

In Step 3 we saw how easy it is to slip into repetitive patterns of thinking that are all too often negative and based on interpretations rather than fact. These negative automatic thoughts can be categorized into various types of *thinking errors*. The table below lists the most common types, with a description and example of each.

Table S4.1

Type of thinking error	Description of thinking error	Example of thinking error
All or nothing	Seeing things as black or white – no shades of grey	I failed my driving test. I am a terrible driver. I will just give up
Over-generalization	One unfortunate event leads to the assumption that this will happen every time.	Every time I eat a biscuit I just know I'll binge
Mental filter	Picking out and dwelling exclusively on the negative/worrying details	Today was a disaster. I had beaten my calorie allowance by lunchtime

Disqualifying the positive	Positive experiences don't count for anything Successes are seen as flukes No pleasure taken from positive events	He only asked me out because he was lonely
Jumping to conclusions	Assuming the worst even when there is no reason to; expecting failure before trying	She didn't speak to me because she could see how fat I was
Catastrophizing	Exaggerating your own imperfections Common misfortunes become disasters	I made a mistake, how awful. I can never show myself here again I will never recover from BN because I binged this morning
Emotional reasoning	Taking feelings as facts (e.g. feeling afraid, therefore there must really be some danger)	I feel fat therefore I am fat
"Should", "must" and "ought" statements	Thinking you should *always* be capable of staying calm or *never* get angry, etc. These statements are overdemanding, unreasonable and cause unnecessary pressure	I should be 8 stones therefore I must diet I ought to be a better daughter
Labelling/ mislabelling	Labelling yourself on the same basis of one mistake	I got that wrong: I'm a useless person
Personalization	Attribute things going wrong to oneself	My parents fight because I'm an awful daughter

Challenging Thinking Errors

Diary 3

Date	Emotions	Situation	Automatic thoughts	Thinking errors
12.5.96	Disgust/ anger at myself	Sitting alone in my room after a binge	I must not eat anything tomorrow to make up for the binge I had tonight	All or nothing
14.5.96	Fear/panic	Sitting in the dining room at lunch	People are staring at me because I am so fat and ugly	Jumping to conclusions
15.5.96	Ashamed Miserable	In a department store trying on a dress	If I can't fit a size 10 I must be overweight I look so fat in this dress I may as well go home	Catastrophizing All or nothing

If we look again at the excerpt from the cognitive therapy diary of the student mentioned in the last Step, we can now add an extra column to the table to identify the thinking errors involved.

With the help of this example, now look back over any negative automatic thoughts that you have recorded and try to decide if these thoughts contain any of the types of thinking errors listed in the table. Write down beside the negative automatic thought which thinking error it contains. Sometimes a thought will fit into more than one category, so don't worry if you can't find just one slot for each of your thoughts.

You will probably find that there are certain patterns of errors you keep on making; in other words, you will have your individual repertoire of habitual thinking errors.

Do not try to think of rational responses to your thinking errors until you have learned to identify the type of error first. This stage is important; in order for rational responses to be effective, it is necessary to understand the negative bias or erroneous thinking that you are trying to challenge.

Summary

- Every negative automatic thought has at least one THINKING ERROR underlying it.
- There are various forms of thinking errors, some of which will be more applicable to you than others.
- Identifying which thinking errors frequently occur for you is a necessary first step on the way to replacing negative automatic thoughts with more rational responses.

Homework assignment for Step 4

- Continue completing your food diary, and working toward the "principles of normal eating".
- This week, every time you record a negative automatic thought in your diary, try to identify the type (or types) of thinking error it represents.
- Try to become aware of the particular kinds of thinking error most common in your own thoughts.

Step 5

Changing Your Eating Patterns

This Step begins with an overview of the effects of AN and dieting on metabolism. People with AN often believe in many myths about changes in weight and what will happen to them if they eat normally; for example, you may have a powerful fear that you will gain weight in a completely uncontrolled way if you relax your strict controls in the tiniest degree.

Having set out the information relating to the possible barriers that may prevent you from making changes to your diet – in particular, how and why normal fluctuations occur in an individual's weight, and the ways in which the body responds to starvation and to a resumption of normal eating – a system of food portions is introduced by which you can begin to regulate your food intake in a manner which is controlled but not rigid.

AN, Dieting and Metabolism

Weight Fluctuations

In studies which have investigated the normal changes in body weight in healthy, free-living individuals, a fluctuation of ±1kg (2.2lb) between consecutive days is common, and fluctuations of ±0.5 kg (1.1lb) very common. In order to understand the reasons for these variations in body weight during short periods, it is worth considering the various components of the human body which can change in size and thus result in change in weight. These are set out in Table S5.1.

Table S5.1

Component of human body	Tissue type	Daily changes in weight when eating a normal diet	Rate of change in weight when dieting
Structural	Bones, ligaments, cartilages, etc.	None	No change
Major energy reserves	Muscle, fat	None	Changes occur slowly over several weeks of dieting
Short-term energy reserves	Glycogen (stored in combination with water) in the liver	Minimal fluctuations of 0.5–1.0kg are common	Responsible for initial rapid loss of weight in first few days of dieting

Although loss of mineral from the bones is a common side-effect of starvation, the effects of this on body weight are small. The body's glycogen stores are specifically designed to provide energy in the short term, i.e. between meals, and in normal circumstances they last only for a few hours. Only when glycogen stores are almost exhausted does the body start to break down muscle and fat stores to release energy.

Figure S5.1 shows what happens when someone does not eat or goes on a very restricted diet. When that person starts to eat or to increase their intake, the diagram will flow in the opposite direction. That is, the excess glucose in the blood will be taken up into the liver in combination with water and stored as glycogen. This may occur either following a binge or when someone increases their diet in a more planned way. In either situation, if weight is checked a rapid increase will be observed, which frequently leads to further dietary restriction in order to reverse the weight gain.

Figure S5.1   **Effects of eating and not eating on energy stores and body weight**

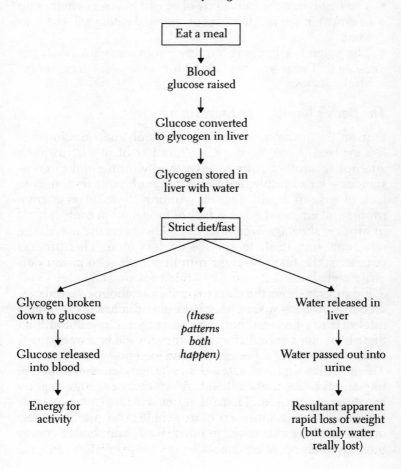

Eat a meal

↓

Blood glucose raised

↓

Glucose converted to glycogen in liver

↓

Glycogen stored in liver with water

↓

Strict diet/fast

Glycogen broken down to glucose

↓

Glucose released into blood

↓

Energy for activity

(these patterns both happen)

Water released in liver

↓

Water passed out into urine

↓

Resultant apparent rapid loss of weight (but only water really lost)

If you look again at the bottom left-hand side of Figure S5.1, you see that burning glycogen gives you energy but no weight loss. The weight loss comes on the right-hand side, but in fact all that is lost is water; and so, as soon as you start to eat again the weight is rapidly regained, even though you have not taken in many calories.

There are two important messages from this analysis for people with eating disorders contemplating dietary changes:

- The first is that the initial rate of weight change (whether up or down) in the first few days of changed eating will not continue.
- The second is that long-term weight maintenance does not mean that your weight has to be the same every time you get on the scales.

The Body's Response to Starvation

During the millions of years over which the human body has evolved it has developed a number of mechanisms to attempt to protect it from adverse environmental circumstances – for example, temperature regulation, responses to lack of oxygen at altitude, etc. Among these adverse environmental circumstances is lack of food, and to protect itself in times of shortage or famine the body lowers the metabolic rate, enabling itself to survive on less food. This process reinforces the fear of weight gain in people who have rigorously dieted.

Figure S5.2 shows the changes in the metabolic rate and subsequently in body weight which occur with changes in energy intake. It can be seen that, when a body is starved and then there is an increase in dietary intake, there will be a weight gain in the short term at a greater rate than for a non-starved person. This short-term gain can be a difficult time, but after a spell of higher intake the metabolic rate and therefore energy requirements are increased. There is no evidence of permanently lowered energy requirements in people who increase their intake following starvation. In other words, your body's energy thermostat always resets itself.

Figure S5.2

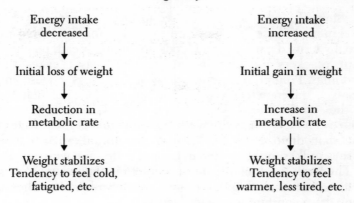

Energy intake decreased	Energy intake increased
↓	↓
Initial loss of weight	Initial gain in weight
↓	↓
Reduction in metabolic rate	Increase in metabolic rate
↓	↓
Weight stabilizes Tendency to feel cold, fatigued, etc.	Weight stabilizes Tendency to feel warmer, less tired, etc.

These processes of decreasing and increasing metabolic rates apply not just to periods of starvation resulting in weight loss, but also to those who starve, binge and vomit at a stable weight. The reduction in metabolic rate is reversed when regular eating patterns are re-established, particularly if food intake is distributed throughout the day.

The Portion System

This section sets out a techniques for regaining control of your eating by applying a "portion" system. The potential benefits of this system for the person attempting to overcome AN are:

- It allows you to remain in control of dietary choice.
- It gives you a flexible alternative to calorie counting.
- It allows a structured but non-rigid pattern of meals.
- It encourages you to introduce "difficult" foods within a planned system.
- It generally leads to a nutritionally adequate range of foods as long as you are not restricting excessively.

What is the Portion System?

A system of food "portions" is used to vary the overall level of food intake. These "portions" are applied primarily to what are usually termed carbohydrate foods, including bread, potatoes, fruit, crackers and biscuits, rice, cereals, pasta, cakes and puddings. Protein foods, such as meat, fish, eggs, cheese and beans, are taken in relatively fixed amounts and are not included in the "portion" total. Vegetables and drinks such as tea and coffee can be taken as you wish, but avoid taking them instead of carbohydrate "portions". Milk (or a suitable alternative, such as soya milk) should be used in tea and coffee and with cereals.

The foods to which the portion system is applied are of variable calorie content, but so long as a variety of foods is chosen each day a constant intake will result.

The following amounts of typical foods each count as one portion:

one slice of bread
two plain biscuits
one chocolate biscuit (digestive etc.)
two oatcakes, crackers etc.
three crispbreads etc.
one bowl of porridge, breakfast cereal
one piece of fruit
one "diet" yogurt
one small potato or scoop of mashed potato
one bowl of soup
two tablespoons of rice
one glass of fruit juice
two tablespoons of pasta

The following amounts of other foods count as two portions:

one bread roll
one greek bread
one large (e.g. baked) potato
one scone, pancake etc.
one croissant
one fruit yogurt

one bag of crisps
one large chocolate biscuit
one individual pudding (rice, custard, tart, pie, etc.)

How Do I Use the Portion System?

To start with, you should try to aim to eat 15 "portions" per day, preferably spread across breakfast, midday meal, evening meal and snacks. It is important to spread the intake of food through the day to avoid feelings of over-fullness, which may make the planned intake difficult to achieve if you try to eat too much at once. You should aim to include a helping of protein-rich food – meat, fish, eggs, cheese or beans – with your midday and evening meals (for example, in a sandwich at midday and as part of the main course in the evening).

Once you have established a regular pattern of meals, adjustments can be made to the total number of "portions" in order to bring about controlled changes in your weight. These adjustments are best made infrequently, i.e. no more than one change every two weeks or so.

Summary

- It is normal for fluctuations in weight to occur daily.
- Establishing a healthy eating pattern allows the body to hold some energy in reserve in the liver in the form of glycogen.
- Water held with this store of glycogen causes an *initial* rise in weight when food intake increases, but this will rapidly stabilize.
- Water released from glycogen and excreted in the urine causes an initial weight loss when you starve for a day. This weight loss is not due to loss of muscle or fat.
- Starvation, even as part of a starve/binge/vomit cycle at a stable weight, leads to a decrease in metabolic rate.
- The reverse happens when a normal healthy eating

(continued on next page)

pattern is resumed – that is, metabolic rate increases again. However, a lag in the rise in metabolic rate results in a further *initial* weight gain, but again this rapidly stabilizes.

- Developing a system of "portions" in your eating plan allows you to remain in control of dietary choice without calorie counting, and gives your body a nutritionally adequate range of food.
- Fifteen "portions", spread over three meals and two snacks, is a good pattern to minimize bloating and break the habit of long periods of fasting.
- The number of portions can then be changed as necessary, in order to alter your average weight.

Homework assignment for Step 5

- Continue completing your food diary and working toward the "principles of normal eating".
- Have a go at implementing the portion system. You will see that there is space in the diary sheets set out in Step 2 to record how many portions you are eating in the first right-hand column headed "Por").
- It is a good idea to attempt all the exercises suggested so far before moving on. If you have been unable to do this, don't worry; just go back and try again. There is no limit on how long you can stay with one Step.
- Remember that no stage in getting back to a normal eating pattern is easy to accomplish. Don't expect miracles from yourself, and don't forget to reward yourself for any achievements you have made, no matter how small.
- When you feel ready to move on, continue with the next treatment section.

Step 6

Improving Your Body Image

AN and Body Image Distortion

"Body image" refers to the mental picture that a person has of her own body. It is therefore based on *how she feels about* her body, and not on its actual physical appearance. People with AN tend to have a very negative body image. Look at Figure S6.1. Do you recognize any of the statements in the diagram as comments you have made about how you feel about your own body?

Figure S6.1 **Body image distortion in AN**

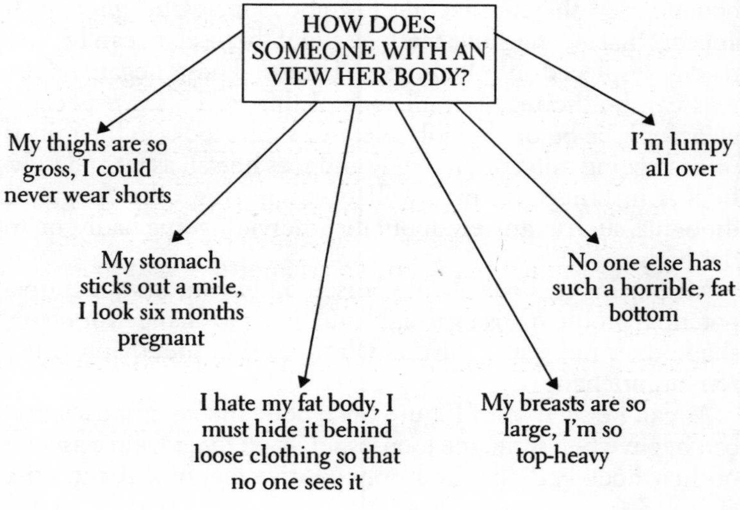

HOW DOES SOMEONE WITH AN VIEW HER BODY?

My thighs are so gross, I could never wear shorts

I'm lumpy all over

My stomach sticks out a mile, I look six months pregnant

No one else has such a horrible, fat bottom

I hate my fat body, I must hide it behind loose clothing so that no one sees it

My breasts are so large, I'm so top-heavy

It is not unusual to mistake strong feelings for facts (e.g. "I *feel* lumpy all over, therefore I must *be* lumpy all over"). This is, however, a thinking error (emotional reasoning; see Table S4.1). These feelings can become so strong that the person becomes convinced that her body actually looks as bad as it feels. The result is *body image distortion*, one of the most distressing features of AN.

Julie, a 25-year-old student, had suffered from AN for two years. When she initially came for help with her eating disorder she had a very distorted body image. Despite being within the normal weight range for someone of her age and height, she was convinced that she looked "pudgy" all over and that her thighs and buttocks were out of proportion to the rest of her body. As she described herself, "I just wobble like a jelly." She could not try on clothes in shops because she felt so ashamed about how she looked and hated places that had numerous mirrors. Whenever she felt down, she dwelt on how fat she was, and whenever she was anxious, e.g. before a job interview, she would get very unhappy and all she could focus on was how awful she looked.

Like Julie, many people with AN tend to feel worse about their bodies when they are feeling low and hopeless in general. It appears that any negative feelings about themselves can be very readily displaced into feelings of fatness. These negative feelings can be the result of all sorts of things. This is especially clear for Julie before her job interviews. She looks in the mirror prior to going into the interview and sees herself as fat and ugly. In this instance she may well be displacing other negative thoughts, such as anxiety about the interview going badly, on to her body.

Misplacing feelings about yourself on to your body sets up a potential problem: losing weight and trying to change your body shape does not really solve anything as the underlying issues remain unchanged.

As can be seen from Figure S6.2, body image dissatisfaction can begin when someone focuses solely on the negative aspects of their body and disregards any positive features. It can arise

Figure S6.2   **Interaction of thinking error and body image distortion**

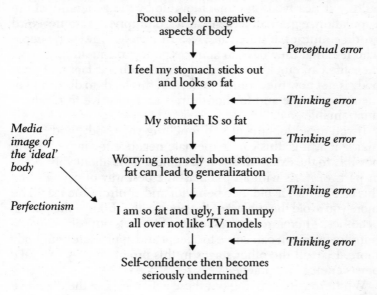

from dissatisfaction with the whole body or with part of the body; in the latter case that dissatisfaction is then generalized over time. The way someone feels about their body is often reflected in how they view themselves as a person. The last stage of Figure S6.2 shows that having a negative or distorted body image may seriously undermine an individual's self-confidence.

Ideal and Reality

Perfectionism can result in a negative body image. The media provide us with an image of the female, in particular, that is portrayed as the "ideal body". This image itself is often a distortion: photographs of models are frequently elongated to make the model look taller and thinner than she really is. Therefore very few people can even approach this ideal body shape. Indeed, some ideas of beauty stress the rarity value of "beauty", and what is considered beautiful or ideal in any particular culture is nearly always unachievable by the generality of the population, e.g. small feet in China, plumpness in some Third World countries, thinness in Western society. However, people who feel that they have to achieve perfection in all aspects of their life can quickly become obsessed with the fact that their body is not how they want it to be, and this leads to distortion of their own image and further distress as they strive to reach an unattainable goal.

If you avoid looking at and touching your body, and recognizing it as it is, this can perpetuate negative feelings about it, possibly to the extent that you become *phobic* about your body, or parts of it. As with all phobias, the best way of overcoming this is to reduce avoidance behavior and confront the fear. The more you avoid the subject of the phobia, the stronger the phobia becomes. Therefore, the rest of this Step sets out some suggestions for ways you can come to accept and appreciate your body more. Like all the other stages in this program, they will take perseverance and practice.

While you are carrying out these activities, use the cognitive techniques you have learnt to challenge thoughts about your body.

Writing Your Body's History

Understanding where your negative body image or even body hatred comes from may help you gradually change it. One way of doing this is to write a history of your body and the way you view this.

- It is probably easiest to do this by taking particular points in time say, at age 5, age 8, age 11 and age 15.
- It is sometimes useful to get out old family photos and use those as triggers to the way you are feeling at the time.
- Sometimes it may be a particular family event or scene which hasn't been captured in a family photo but which you can remember clearly. Try and think back to a time when you felt comfortable about your body and start here.

- If you are looking at a family photo, ask yourself where am I standing in relation to other family members? Do I look happy or sad? Do I look part of the group, or am I alone? Is the family including or excluding me? What was going on in the family at this time? How was I feeling about myself and my body?
- Do this for each page and write a story of how your negative body image developed.
- Don't stop at the point at which your AN has developed. If there are photos after that, include these and ask yourself the same questions.

Learning to accept or even like your body again is not going to be easy. It is going to take a lot of time and a lot of repetition of small simple tasks. Here are some things that may help.

Re-writing the story. Re-write your story as though you hadn't developed a negative body image. What would have been different? Would you have been more effective at changing things within the family? Would relationships have worked out differently? This may be hard to do and it may feel unbelievable, but try and persevere. Anything which puts different ideas, alternatives, in your mind may help.

Create an alternative body image (schema). Make this a kind, warm, benevolent compassionate "you". One that is not critical of you, not judgmental, less perfectionistic. Take this other "you" around with you. Imagine it sitting on your shoulder or standing behind you. When you have negative body experiences, listen to what it has to say about you and the way you are.

Try to disregard the media. Not all women with AN develop their problem because of media images or media pressure, but some do. Remember that we live in a very distorted world. Images that you see in magazines and on TV are frequently unreal. They are photographed in certain ways with particular lighting, they are often air brushed and sometimes vertically distorted. You may have had the experience of seeing someone famous and being surprised at how much shorter and dumpier they actually looked in real life compared with on the screen. Repeatedly say to yourself when you see these images: this is not reality this is a distortion.

Keep a positive diary. Your body image has been maintained by thousands of occasions when you have said to yourself something critical about your body or negatively compared yourself with others. Anorexia nervosa causes you to focus on these negative aspects and miss out the positive ones. Try and experiement for a week, only noting down positive or pleasurable experiences you have in relation to your body and ignoring the negative ones. This will help you correct the bias that is built into your thinking.

Body Image Activities

The following suggested activities may help you to think more about your body image distortion and focus on why this may have come about. For each exercise, set aside some time when you know that you will not be required to do anything else and will have peace and quiet. You may find it helps to work through each one on paper. It is a good idea to use a notebook – it could be the same one in which you keep your food diaries, or a different one – to record your thoughts and feelings as you work through these exercises; you will then have the notes readily to hand and can refer back to them when you want to in the future.

1 Try to imagine yourself in 10 or 20 years' time. Where are you and what are you doing? What are your aims and ambitions? Ask yourself if you are on track for achieving these goals, or if you need to make changes. Write your goals down, and look at them when you are low and in need of a focus.

2 Now look at who you are now. Ask yourself how you see yourself, and write this down. Then ask yourself how you think you are seen by others, and write this down. Compare the two. What are the differences and what are the similarities? Turn over on to a new page. Consider how you would like to see yourself, and how you would like to be seen by others.

Write both down. What would need to be changed in order for you to be seen as you would like, both by yourself and by others? How would you go about making such change or changes?

3 Think of some woman who impresses you yet is not excessively thin. It may be a relative, a friend, an actress, a sportswoman, a businesswoman . . . What is it that impresses you – that makes you notice and respect her? It could, for example, be style, posture, confidence, energy, vivaciousness, intelligence, sense of control and purpose, or any one or more of a number of things. Ask yourself if you have any of these qualities; if not, think what you could do to cultivate them. Do you think weight and shape are of such importance to the person you respect? If not, what do you think is likely to be important to her?

4 Stand in front of a mirror and look at your body. For each negative statement you come up with about your reflection, make yourself say something positive – even if you do not believe it yet. Write these positive affirmations down and practise repeating them when you find yourself criticizing your body. Though this will feel quite forced to start with, try to persevere.

5 Does your body image restrict you in any way? Are there some things you avoid doing? Examples may be looking in a full-length mirror, wearing a bikini on holiday, trying on clothes in a communal changing room, using communal showers, etc. Write a list of these and make a resolution to try to confront rather than avoid these uncomfortable situations. Try to do these things and see if you can think differently. For example, when changing in a communal changing room, or sunbathing on holiday, look at other women's bodies. Are they perfect? Would you swap? Usually the answer will be no. Be critical: think of a reason why you prefer your body to theirs; remember this, and record it in your notebook.

6 Pamper yourself physically. Though you may be in a pattern of being critical about yourself, take time to look after what you do have. Treat yourself to a long, luxurious, hot bath and

afterwards spend time massaging aromatic oils into your skin from head to toe. Take time to linger on each part of your anatomy and try to counterbalance each negative thought with a positive one. If you think "My thighs are so fat and flabby," set against this "My skin feels so soft and smooth." Put on some nail polish, have a make-over, try a new hair style or shade. Make the effort to be kind to yourself, and try hard to stop being habitually self-critical.

7 Let's talk exercise. Do you do exercise for pleasure – or out of guilt and anxiety? What is exercise *for*? For your pleasure, enjoyment and fulfilment? Or to burn calories and fat and make you thinner? I suggest it may be the latter. If so, try to think of something you would actively *enjoy* doing: if you really do want to be physically active, perhaps a dance class, or aqua-aerobics; or it could be something less strenuous, such as seeing films, visiting art galleries, reading novels. The important thing is to allocate time for activities you genuinely *enjoy*. If it helps, write down a selection of possibilities and score them on a scale of 1–10 for enjoyment. Make the effort to give highest priority to the ones you think will give you most enjoyment.

Breaking the Cycle

As you try to break the cycle of body image distortion and renewed urges to eat less and get thinner, ask yourself the following questions. They may help you to be more aware of the patterns of thought that have become habitual to you, and of *why* you think the way you do, and so help you to begin to break the automatic connection between perceived/distorted body image and self-esteem that reinforces the symptoms of AN.

• Try to identify the times when you feel worst about your body. Are you in fact misplacing other problems on to your body? What might these underlying issues be? Boredom? Anxiety? Anger? Try to identify what is really troubling you.

- Many people have described the onset of their dieting as being associated with a feeling of being "out of control" of some aspect to their life. Dieting to them felt like something that they could control, and this was a relief at the time. Is there anything in your life that feels out of your control, and is increasing the urge to control your body weight by way of compensating for this?
- Is your body image distortion making the problem worse?
- Are you seeing only the negative aspects of your shape and forgetting the rest of your body?
- Could you see your body more positively? Try not to focus on body parts that you are dissatisfied with. See your body as a whole.

The key point is to try to break the connection between how you view yourself *as a person* and how you visualize *your body*.

Summary

- People who suffer from AN tend to have a very negative body image, i.e. they *feel* that parts of themselves are much fatter and uglier than they really are, and they translate this feeling into a belief that *they are* fat and ugly.
- A person with AN often has a view of herself as a person that is strongly influenced, if not dominated, by her feelings about her body, which severely undermines her self-confidence.
- Perfectionism can lead to a negative body image and much misery while striving for the unobtainable goal of the "perfect" body.
- For someone suffering from AN, general negative feelings, e.g. feelings of hopelessness or depression, can readily be displaced into feelings of fatness.
- Avoiding looking at or touching your body perpetuates negative thoughts and feelings about it.

Homework assignment for Step 6

- Continue with your diary as before.
- Look back through the diaries you have amassed over the past few weeks, and ask yourself the following questions:
  - What connections are there between eating and feelings?
  - What are your automatic thoughts about weight, shape and food?
  - Do the same thoughts tend to keep cropping up?
  - Are you able to challenge any of these thoughts?
  - If you are able to challenge them, does it make any difference to your behavior?
  - Which of the various coping strategies presented in the manual so far are you finding helpful to you?
- Try to work through all the activities 1–7 on body image listed above and write your body history (see p.134). This may be quite draining for you, but do try to persevere; they may well give you a lot of useful information.
- If you have been unable to carry out these exercises so far, don't worry; go back and read through them again, and have another go.
- When you feel ready, continue with the next treatment section.

Step 7

Developing Assertiveness

For someone with AN, the rationale behind learning to be more assertive is that it may provide you with a tool other than food avoidance to get what you want. Learning to be assertive requires practice, and it is not easy to teach by way of a self-help manual. However, the information presented here can be used as a set of guidelines which you can experiment with, to give you a starting point on which you can build as you gain in confidence.

What is Assertiveness?

What does "being assertive" mean? To start with, it may be useful to review a "Bill of Assertiveness Rights", taken from Manuel J. Smith's book *When I Say No, I Feel Guilty*:

1 You have the right to judge your own behavior, thoughts and emotions and to take the responsibility for their initiation and consequences upon yourself.
2 You have the right to offer no reasons or excuses for justifying your behavior.
3 You have the right to judge if you are responsible for finding solutions to other people's problems.
4 You have the right to change your mind.
5 You have the right to make mistakes – and be responsible for them.
6 You have the right to say, "I don't know."
7 You have the right to be independent of the goodwill of others before coping with them.

8 You have right to be "illogical" in making decisions.
9 You have the right to say, "I don't understand."
10 You have the right to say, "I don't care."

In any form of communication, be it verbal or non-verbal, there are three different ways to act:

- assertive;
- aggressive;
- non-assertive.

So what differentiates these three different types of behavior?

Assertion

As you can see from Figure S7.1, assertive behavior involves standing up for your own rights – expressing your thoughts, feelings and beliefs in a way which

- is direct, honest and appropriate, and
- does not violate the rights of another person.

It involves respect, not submission. You are respecting your own needs and rights as well as accepting that the other person also has needs and rights.

Figure S7.1 **Assertive, aggressive and non-assertive behavior**

Assertive		Stands up for your own personal rights
		Does not violate the other person's rights

Aggressive		Stands up for your own personal rights
		Violates the rights of the other person

Non-assertive		Does not stand up for your own personal rights
		Allows another person to violate your rights

Aggression

This involves standing up for personal rights and expressing your own thoughts, feelings and beliefs in a way which

- is often dishonest and usually inappropriate, and
- always violates the rights of the other person.

The usual goal of aggression is domination and winning, forcing the other person to lose. Winning is ensured by humiliating or overpowering other people so that they become weaker and less able to express and defend their needs and rights. The message is:

- This is what I think – you're stupid for believing differently.
- This is what I want – what you want isn't important.
- This is what I feel – your feelings don't count.

Non-Assertion

This involves not standing up for your own rights by

- not expressing honest feelings, thoughts and beliefs, and thereby
- letting others violate your personal rights.

The message communicated is:

- I don't count – you can take advantage of me.
- My feelings don't matter – only yours do.
- I'm nothing – you're superior.

So, it means you are not respecting your own rights and needs. The goal of non-assertion is to appease others and avoid conflict at any cost.

Different Responses in the Same Scenario

Figure S7.2 shows three different possible responses to a single scenario: one aggressive, one assertive, one non-assertive. The following exercise will help to clarify what we mean by the words

A Self-Help Manual

Figure S7.2 **Assertive, aggressive and non-assertive responses**

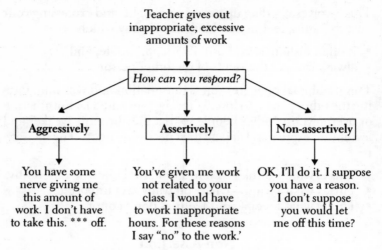

"assertive", "non-assertive" and "aggressive", consolidate the different types of responses available to you and help you to see which type you routinely use.

For each situation, make suggestions for what you think the three types of responses might be: i.e. not how you would behave under the circumstances, but how you think an aggressive, non-assertive or assertive person might respond.

(a) You are out for a works night out in mixed company. During a friendly difference of opinion one of the men says quite seriously, "Of course women are definitely the inferior race. It's been proved."

Aggressive: _____

_____

Non-assertive: _____

_____

Assertive: _____

_____

(b) You are with friends deciding which movie you are all going to see. Someone suggests a movie which you have already seen and didn't like at all.

Aggressive: _____

_____

Non-assertive: _____

_____

Assertive: _____

_____

(c) A colleague from work criticizes another mutual colleague. You feel the criticism is unjustified:

Aggressive: _____

_____

Non-assertive: _____

_____

Assertive: _____

_____

(d) You bought an expensive designer dress that you really liked. After the first wash the stitching around the left shoulder seam started to come undone.

Aggressive: _____

_____

Non-assertive: _____

_____

Assertive: _____

_____

(e) You return a pair of trousers because the stitching is faulty. It was the only pair of trousers in that style that were your size. The assistant offers you an exchange or a credit note.

Aggressive: _____

_____

Non-assertive: _____

_____

Assertive: _____

_____

(f) You have whizzed home during your lunch break and are quickly eating a bowl of soup before rushing back to work. The door bell rings and a smartly dressed man, saying that he is from the gas company, asks to be let in to check your piping as part of a safety campaign. You have had no warning of this and are in a hurry to get back to work.

Aggressive: _____

_____

Non-assertive: _____

_____

Assertive: _____

_____

(g) You have gone to a newly opened restaurant for lunch. They are very slow to take your order and when your food arrives, it is cold.

Aggressive: _____

_____

Non-assertive: _____

_____

Assertive: _____

_____

Now look back over your answers and note, for each case,

- which response of the three you would normally use, and
- which one you feel is most appropriate in the situation. Imagine yourself as the person at the receiving end of your statement and see which response feels the most comfortable.

Reasons for Acting Assertively

- *Why be assertive rather than non-assertive?* Non-assertive people often fear losing the respect of others. However, non-assertion does not guarantee approval. People may pity rather than approve of non-assertion, and this pity can eventually turn into irritation and finally into disgust or contempt.
- *Why be assertive rather than aggressive?* Aggression does not guarantee successful control over other people. It just means they will probably go "underground" with their feelings. Assertive behavior increases your feelings of "self-control" and makes you feel more confident. Aggression will probably make you feel more vulnerable. Assertion rather than aggression results in closer relationships with others. You won't necessarily win, but both parties can at least partially achieve some goals and get their needs met.

Assertive behavior increases your own self-respect, leading to greater self-confidence and thus reducing the need for others' approval. Usually, people respect and admire those who are responsibly assertive, showing respect for self and others. Assertion results in individuals having their needs satisfied and preferences respected.

Types of Assertion

Now that we can differentiate assertive behavior from aggressive and non-assertive, we need to look to different types of assertion and when to use them.

Figure S7.3   **The five types of assertion**

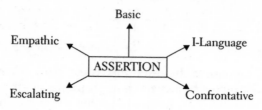

Figure S7.3 shows five different types of assertion, each of which suits a different situation. We will now look at each one in greater depth and give examples to show the type of situation in which it is most appropriately used.

Basic Assertion

This is expressing basic personal rights, beliefs or feelings, e.g.

- When being asked an important question for which you are unprepared: "I'd like to have a few minutes to think that over."
- When it is apparent you don't need advice: "I don't want any more advice."
- Also, expressing affection and appreciation to others: "I like you." "I care for you a lot." "You're someone special to me."

Empathic Assertion

This is expressing your needs/feelings, but also showing sensitivity to the other person, e.g.

- When two people are chatting loudly while a meeting is in progress: "You may not realize it, but your talking is starting to make it hard for me to hear what's going on in the meeting. Would you keep it down."
- When having some furniture delivered: "I know it's hard to say when the truck will come, but I would like an estimate of the arrival time."

Escalating Assertion

This starts with a minimal assertive response, usually achieving the goal with minimum of effort. When the other person fails to respond and continues to violate your rights, you gradually increase the assertion and become increasingly firm without becoming aggressive. For example, say you are in a bar with a friend and a man repeatedly offers to buy you drinks.

- Your first response is: "That's very nice of you to offer, but we're here to catch up on some news. Thanks anyway."
- Next time you say: "No thank you. We really would rather talk to each other."
- Finally you say: "This is the third and last time I am going to tell you we don't want your company. Please leave."

The final, blunt refusal was *appropriate* because the earlier assertions were ignored.

Confrontative Assertion

This is used when the other person's words contradict what he/she does. This type of assertion involves describing what the other person said would be done, what they actually did, and what you want done, e.g.

- "I said it was OK to borrow my CDs as long as you checked with me first. Now you're borrowing them without asking. I'd like to know why you did that."

I-Language Assertion

This is assertively expressing difficult negative feelings. e.g.

- "When your half of the desk is so messy, I start feeling angry and that upsets me. I'd like you to be more neat and organized."
- "When I'm constantly interrupted, I lose my train of thought and begin to feel that my ideas are not important to me. I start feeling hurt and angry. I'd like you to make a point of waiting until I've finished speaking."

Use of Assertion

If behaving assertively is new to you, you might find it helpful to use Figure S7.4 to formulate a basic plan of how you are going to approach each new situation.

Figure S7.4 **An approach to behaving assertively**

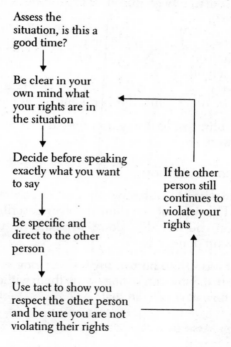

If, to begin with, you don't feel confident enough to behave assertively with everyone, then try doing some role-playing with a close friend at home before launching the new, assertive you on the rest of the world.

> *Beccie, a 27-year-old office worker, had suffered from AN for five years. She had low self-esteem and was very miserable both at home and at work. After a hard day at work she came home to start the cooking, cleaning and ironing, running after the*

children and her husband. The list of tasks was endless. She was unable to see any way out, feeling that it was her duty to do all this work and feeling guilty for moaning about it. Occasionally she felt like screaming at her husband for help but was scared of what he might do in response.

A friend suggested that Beccie join an assertiveness class with her. She decided to go along although she was doubtful that it would help. She was taught about "The Bill of Assertiveness Rights" and how to act assertively, practising in class by role-playing. Soon she began to realize that looking after the home was not her sole responsibility and that it was acceptable to ask her family for help. Her family put up some resistance initially as they did not like having to do "extra" work, but she prodded them along, using her new-found assertive techniques. Soon Beccie found that life was somewhat easier and more enjoyable.

Why Don't People Act Assertively?

Reasons Why People Act Non-Assertively

Like Beccie in the case history described above, you may have more than one reason why you don't act assertively. In her case it was a combination of failure to accept that she had personal rights, and anxiety about the negative consequences. Once she became convinced that she did have rights and feelings, that she was entitled to just as much consideration as any other human being, she was able to act more assertively, at which point she found that the negative consequences were not as bad as she had feared.

Other reasons for acting non-assertively are:

- Mistaking firm assertion for aggression.
- Mistaking non-assertion for politeness . . . but is it polite, or is it actually dishonest?
- Mistaking non-assertion for being helpful, when it really is exactly the opposite!
- Poor social skills. This is where role-playing can be particularly helpful, allowing you to practise assertion in safe surroundings.

If you are frequently non-assertive, you will feel a growing loss of self-esteem, and an increasing sense of hurt and anger. Internal tension may result (as with Beccie). Close relationships can be difficult without honest expression of thoughts and feelings. Other people may feel irritation about the non-assertive person, leading to a lack of respect.

Reasons Why People Act Aggressively

- Out of powerlessness and a feeling of being under threat.
- As an extreme counter-reaction to previous non-assertion.
- In over-reaction due to past emotional experiences.
- Because of mistaken beliefs about aggression, i.e. that this is the only way to get through.
- Through not knowing how to be assertive.

If you are frequently aggressive, you might lose or fail to establish close relationships and feel that you have to be constantly on the watch for counter-attacks. You might lose your job, miss out on promotion, develop high blood pressure, and feel misunderstood and unloved; and you may feel guilt, shame or embarrassment after your aggression.

Summary

- *Assertion* involves standing up for your own personal rights while not violating those of others.
- *Non-assertion* allows others to violate your personal rights and may lead to them losing respect and pitying you.
- *Aggression* violates the rights of others and does not guarantee successful control over them.
- Assertive behavior increases your own self-respect, leading to greater self-confidence and thus reducing the need for others' approval.
- There are several types of assertion; to maximize the impact of any of them it is important to use timing and tact.
- Role-playing is a good way of increasing your confidence in using assertive behavior before trying it out in the "real" world.

Homework assignment for Step 7

- Continue your diary as before.
- Review last week's diary. Identify situations in which you are not assertive. Write them down. In what way are you not assertive in each situation? How could you be more assertive in each situation?
- Practise being more assertive in the situations you have identified as being problematic. Record the results of your more assertive behavior, and compare them with when you are less assertive. How does it feel to be more assertive?
- Changing your behavior from aggressive or non-assertive to assertive can be a difficult and slow task. Remember that it has probably taken you years to perfect your present behavior, so it will take rather more than a day to change it!
- An important first step is to recognize the three types of behavior and which one you most commonly use. If you have not managed this yet, *don't worry*; work through the step again at your own pace until you feel comfortable with it.
- When you feel ready, continue with the next treatment section.

Step 8

Dealing with Anxiety

It has been calculated that as many as 70 per cent of women with anorexia nervosa also experience some type of anxiety disorder at some stage. Anxiety can have significant effects on your quality of life, as the following example shows.

> *Megan, a 25-year-old shop assistant, had been suffering from AN for seven years. She hated going out to parties, but her friends always nagged her to go and she was afraid she would look "different" if she refused.*

> *On the days leading up to a party she would find herself becoming irritable and edgy, worrying excessively about what to wear, what she would say and what others would think of her. At the parties themselves, she found herself to be sweating profusely and often felt others would hear her heart beating, it was so loud. She was always exhausted and miserable by the time she arrived back home.*

Overcoming anxiety involves first understanding the causes and symptoms.

Figure S8.1 shows the many ways in which anxiety and AN interact. Are you a stress eater (turning to food for comfort, grazing, etc.) or a stress dieter?

Symptoms of Anxiety

The effects of anxiety can be felt as physical sensations, as in Megan's case, described above. These physical effects are very

Figure S8.1 **AN and anxiety**

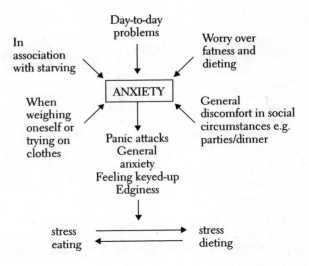

real and are determined by the body's automatic response to perceived danger, whereby the body prepares itself for "fight or flight" in the face of perceived danger by raising the heart rate, quickening breathing and producing adrenaline. Problems arise when this reaction occurs in a situation which would not normally call for such a dramatic response, i.e. in an *inappropriate* setting.

Hyperventilation, or "overbreathing", can itself produce a range of frightening sensations which may trigger a continuous rise in anxiety and thus further symptoms. For this reason, if you find yourself hyperventilating, it is worth learning how to calm your breathing. Other books in this series deal with the causes and symptoms of anxiety in greater depth and contain useful suggestions on counteracting symptoms: see *Overcoming Anxiety* by Helen Kennerley, *Overcoming Panic* by Derrick Silove and Vijaya Manicavasagar and *Overcoming Social Anxiety and Shyness* by Gillian Butler. (For details see the "Useful Books" section on p. 183.)

Figure S8.2   **The physical effects of anxiety**

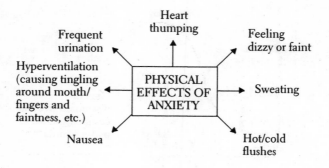

Figure S8.3   **Anxiety-induced changes in thinking**

Anxiety can also produce changes in your thinking, again as we saw with Megan, who found herself to be irritable and edgy before social events. Figure S8.3 shows some of the other effects of anxiety on thinking.

Figure S8.4   **How anxiety levels change over time**

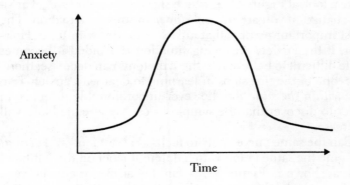

Figure S8.5   **How anorexic feelings about food change over time**

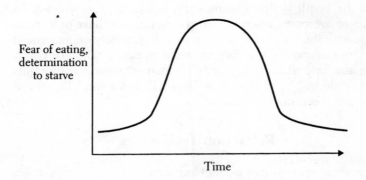

Looking at Figures S8.2 and S8.3 and Megan's case history, think about your own experience of anxiety:

- Note down any symptoms, either mentioned above, or any others that you have experienced, which you think may be attributed to anxiety.
- Have you ever had a panic attack? If so, what physical and psychological symptoms occur for you?
- What does anxiety feel like to you?

Anxiety and Eating

Take a look at Figure S8.4, which shows how your level of anxiety changes if you are in, and *stay in*, a stressful situation. The most important point is that anxiety subsides with time. However, if the anxiety-provoking situation is avoided it becomes quite difficult to believe that the symptoms can decrease; therefore, one of the first steps in learning to deal with anxiety is to *stay within the situation*, however uncomfortable it seems, in order to discover that the symptoms can be tolerated and will decrease.

Can the same curve apply to feelings about food and eating? Imagine the same graph with a different label on the left-hand axis, as shown in Figure S8.5 – and the answer is clearly "yes". Again, it can be difficult to believe that these feelings are tolerable; the easiest option seems to be to "give in" and avoid eating. But this could in fact be described as *avoiding* the anxiety; and the result is that the anorexic behavior is reinforced. In order to overcome anorexic symptoms you may have to learn to cope with the increasing tension by using anxiety management techniques and finding distractions from eating-related anxiety. It is also important to tackle the negative automatic thoughts that could trigger a binge; refer back to Steps 3 and 4 to remind yourself about how to do this.

Relaxation Techniques

Increasing tension can be tackled directly by using relaxation techniques. Relaxation can also be used to develop an awareness of physical tension that may build up to the point where it becomes problematic.

To begin with, it may be useful to use one of the many relaxation tapes commercially available. These will take you through a sequence of stages, prompting you to relax the main muscle groups of the body in turn and often inviting you to imagine yourself in a safe, relaxing situation, e.g. in a sunny garden or on a private beach. Figure S8.6 sets out some guidelines for using such a tape.

Figure s8.6 **How to approach a relaxation exercise**

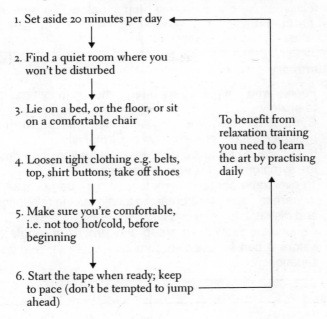

1. Set aside 20 minutes per day

2. Find a quiet room where you won't be disturbed

3. Lie on a bed, or the floor, or sit on a comfortable chair

4. Loosen tight clothing e.g. belts, top, shirt buttons; take off shoes

5. Make sure you're comfortable, i.e. not too hot/cold, before beginning

6. Start the tape when ready; keep to pace (don't be tempted to jump ahead)

To benefit from relaxation training you need to learn the art by practising daily

Remember:

- Concentrate on breathing slowly, smoothly and evenly, and not too deeply, throughout the exercises.
- Practise relaxation only when there is no time pressure – not, for example, 15 minutes before you are due to leave for work.
- As daily practice is crucial, set aside a regular time each day for your relaxation exercises, e.g. after work, after your evening meal or just before going to bed. Do not just use the tape when you feel a bit anxious. Outside your practice times the tape may be used as often as you wish.
- Using the tape is a training phase. Once you have learned and are comfortable with the relaxation exercises, you will be in a position to use relaxation to combat anxiety in "real-life" situations.

Other suggestions of ways to relax, including how to make your own relaxation tape, are given in Step 10 below, "Coping Strategies for the Future".

Summary

- People who have AN very often suffer from symptoms of anxiety.
- Symptoms can be *physical* e.g. palpitations, hyperventilation, or *emotional* e.g. irritability.
- If you *stay in* an anxiety-provoking situation, with time the symptoms of anxiety will decrease.
- To overcome anorexic symptoms it may be necessary to learn to cope with increasing tension using relaxation and distraction techniques.
- Relaxation must be *learned* and *practised* regularly before it can be used to combat anxiety in "real-life" situations.

Homework assignment for Step 8

- Continue your diary as before.
- Remember the "principles of normal eating".
- Practise relaxation (if possible using a relaxation tape), taking care to follow the instructions given in Figure S8.6.
- Learning relaxation techniques can be very worthwhile in helping you to overcome your eating disorder. If you have not managed to practise relaxation regularly so far, then decide right now what time of the day is easiest for you to set aside for relaxation practice and make sure that you use that time solely for that purpose. Spend a few days practising the technique before moving on.
- If you feel that you have managed to grasp the basics of a relaxation technique, then in your own time, turn over the page to start the next step.

Step 9

Managing Your Relationships

Neither you nor your AN exists in a vacuum, and it is important to consider how family, friends and work relationships are entangled in your situation. Interpersonal difficulties may be involved in the development and maintenance of the disorder and in preventing you from recovering; whether or not your close relationships have anything to do with the development of your eating disorder, they will almost inevitably be markedly affected by the fact that you have AN. This step is designed to help you understand your personal relationships and to manage them effectively.

Stage I: An Interpersonal Map

Draw a map which includes all your interpersonal relationships. An example is given in Figure S9.1. Think of all the people you interact with and include them in the map: family, friends, those involved in treating you. It need not be limited to humans; include pets if you have them, as they can be significant in your life. It may be useful to include the AN itself, if you experience it as an entity with which you have a relationship. Sometimes it is useful to draw separate maps, one for before your AN began and one for afterwards.

Once you have done this, set the map aside for a day or two and then go back to it again. You may be surprised to find that you have overlooked important relationships that you can now add.

Why Draw an Interpersonal Map?

1 It helps you to summarize all your relationships on one page.
2 It presents your relationships in picture form.
3 It may help you identify what relationships you want to try and change.

How to Draw an Interpersonal Map

1 Make a list of all your important relationships. Think of all your different social settings, home, school or work and recreation. Include pets if they are important. Include good, bad and distant relationships – any that are important.
2 Begin by putting yourself in the middle of the map.
3 Add each person's name in a circle. The closer the relationship the closer to you, in the middle, that circle should be.
4 Indicate the intensity of the relationship with multiple lines.
5 Indicate the direction of the relationship with arrows, e.g.
  $\longrightarrow$ mainly my giving
  $\longleftarrow$ mainly me receiving
  $\longleftrightarrow$ balanced
6 Try out different versions of the map – pick one that feels right for you:
  a) How I would like my interpersonal world to be
  b) How my interpersonal world was before my AN
  c) How my interpersonal world might be now, without AN
  d) How my interpersonal world will be in ten years if my AN stays the same.
7 Notice the differences, and set yourself goals for the relationship you would like to try and alter.
8 Show the maps to those who are important in your life and get their comments.

Comments on Sally's Maps

In the first map, as things are now:

- Sally has included her AN as a relationship. Currently it is the most powerful and closest relationship she has.
- She would like to have a more equal and balanced relation-

Figure S9.1 **Sally's first map – as she sees it now**

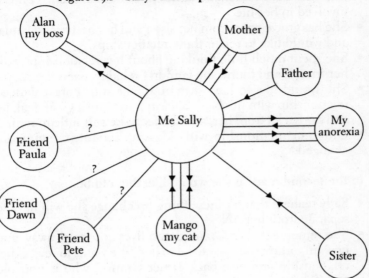

Figure S9.1 **Sally's second map – as she would like it**

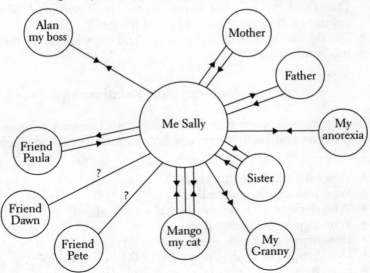

ship with her mother and father, with both of them a bit less involved in her life

- She has grown apart from her sister and her best friend Paula, and would like to repair these relationships.
- She spent much time thinking about her relationships with her friends and found she couldn't reliably assess them.
- She would like to have a more direct and more balanced relationship with her boss. She supports him a great deal, he demands a lot from her, and she feels she gets little in return.
- Only her relationship with Mango, her cat, remains unchanged.

In the second map, as she would like them to be:

- Sally realizes that for these things to change she will have to separate from her AN.
- She remembers her Granny, who lives 400 miles away, and how important she used to be to her. She wants to revive that relationship and give back to her Granny, who is now old and ill.
- She decides to suspend judgment on her relationships with Dawn and Peter, about whom she still feels confused. She needs to gather more evidence and feedback.
- She decides to confide in her sister, and to try to change that relationship first.

Stage 2: Examining Your Relationships

Now, working through your relationship map, take each relationship in turn and begin to examine it. Ask yourself questions such as:

- How often do I see this person?
- Who initiates the contact?
- Who decides what we do or what we talk about?
- Who terminates the contact?
- How happy am I with the frequency of contact?
- How happy am I with the quality of this relationship?
- How balanced or mutual does it feel? (Is it a relationship

where I feel I give but don't receive, or a relationship where
I take and give little?)
- How would I like this relationship to be?
- Do I want to increase the frequency of contact or decrease
it?
- Do I want to alter the nature or intensity of contact?
- Am I happy leaving things just as they are?

Obviously, going through each relationship asking all these
questions may take quite a time – but it is an exercise that is
worth doing.

If you feel stuck, you can ask questions about the whole of
your interpersonal network, such as:

- If I suddenly became ill, who would I turn to for help?
- If I wanted to borrow money at very short notice, who would
I ask?
- If I wanted to confide in someone, who would I choose?
- If I wanted practical advice, who would I choose?

You should now have a very rich picture of your interpersonal
world. If you have done the whole exercise twice, once for the
map before you developed AN and once for the map with AN,
you should also have a clearer picture of how your eating disorder has altered and interacts with your relationships.

You should also have some idea of how you would like your
interpersonal world to be and how balanced your network of
personal relationships is. People differ markedly in what sort of
network they feel comfortable with, but in general a reasonably
wide pattern involving home, work and social activity, with different levels of intensity and closeness in each of those areas, is
best at protecting you from loss, stress and the development of
psychological disorders.

Stage 3: Testing Out Your Analysis

Now you can continue examining your relationships in practice, as both participant and observer. Taking each relationship
in turn, try to monitor what happens the next time you have

contact. Use the questions above to explore how the contact went. Try to behave as naturally as possible and not to alter things. If it is difficult both to take part and to observe, then set aside some time afterwards to go through what happened. Pick a specific and time-limited period of contact to examine, rather than looking globally at the whole relationship.

Were your predictions about the relationship correct? If not, what aspects were different and what surprised you? Remember that at this stage you are not trying to change things, just to get as detailed and accurate a picture as you can of how your relationships actually work.

It may take you some time to gather the evidence you need. Some relationships, though important, may involve quite infrequent contact.

Stage 4: Deciding What to Change and When

Once you have got a complete picture, take some time to consider which relationships you would like to change, which are the most important ones to change and which ones you think you have the most chance of altering. At this stage be quite optimistic; don't assume that certain relationships will be impossible to shift.

For each, consider what part you play in maintaining the current relationship and how much you are prepared to change.

At this point, you may ask: Why bother changing? There are two very important reasons.

- First, having a rich, balanced, safe and supportive network of relationships is one of the most important ways of maintaining your well-being and your psychological health. Research from many different areas and in many different disorders shows that having a good social network and supportive but balanced interpersonal relationships is an excellent protective against adversity.
- Second, one of the themes that run through this book is that AN is centrally linked with beliefs and feelings about control. If you feel in control of your life, your future, your

relationships, it will be easier to give up your AN. If you feel out of control, overwhelmed, intruded upon, then AN can seem your best option. Trying to make some shifts in your relationships may help this sense of control. It is important to emphasize that this is not about *being controlling in* your relationships; you have to play your part in being open and balanced.

Stage 5: Starting to Make Changes

There are two main ways of doing this.

- You can start to make small changes and monitor what happens. For example, if you have decided you would like more contact with your grandmother, start to make more regular phone calls and monitor how things go. Even if it is a relationship that you have previously given up on, if you would like it to be rekindled, then have another go. If it's a relationship with a friend where your assessment has been that you give a great deal and receive very little back, try setting some limits. Start occasionally saying "no". Again, monitor what happens.
- The second way is to put all your cards on the table. Gather all the information you have learned about one relationship and try to discuss this with the individual involved. Be open and not too challenging about this. Use statements such as "This is the way I see things", and ask questions such as "Have I got it right?" "Is your view different?" Obviously this is easier to do when you increase rather than decrease intensity and frequency of contact, and it is also more appropriate when the relationship is one in your close interpersonal circle, e.g. a partner, parent etc.

Summary

- Interpersonal relationships are an extremely important aspect of human life, and a full, balanced network of relationships is a very good way of protecting your well-being.

(continued on next page)

- Whether or not difficulties in particular relationships are involved in your developing AN, those around you will almost certainly be significantly affected by your having this disorder.
- Improving your personal relationships will help your self-confidence and sense of control, and thereby help to make it easier for you to recover from AN.

Homework assignment for Step 9

- Continue to keep your food diary and to work towards the "principles of normal eating".
- Work through the five-stage plan outlined in this Step. You may find it helpful to refer back to Step 7 on "Developing Assertiveness" in working out how to approach and talk to the individuals in your circle.
- If you find it very stressful to approach individuals openly, as described in the second option in Stage 5, try the anxiety management techniques outlined in Step 8; or try using the first option until you feel confident enough to tackle direct discussion.
- Draw your interpersonal maps and practise different versions of these.

Coping Strategies for the Future

The fluctuating nature of AN means that you will experience relapses during self-help or professional treatment. One of the themes of cognitive behavioral therapy is that it is not a cure – for AN or any other disorder – but a set of skills that you will learn during therapy and which you should continue to apply when active therapy is over. This applies to skills learned through self-help, and includes strategies for coping with setbacks. It is not defeatist to expect relapses, only realistic, and you are more likely to overcome these difficulties if you have prepared ways of coping with them in advance.

Preparing for Crisis Moments

Donna, a 35-year-old housewife, had suffered from AN for four years before seeking help. She had been shown the "principles of normal eating" but although in theory she found them very sensible, she found it very difficult to put them into practice. She had been able, in the cold light of day, to sit down and write rational alternatives to her negative automatic thoughts but in the heat of the moment often lapsed back into her old ways.

Look back at the anxiety curve which relates to the increasing urge to starve (Figures S8.4 and S8.5, p. 157). Imagine yourself in a situation where you have a very strong urge not to eat what everyone else is eating – or anything at all. You may feel you need to stay in control, and that if you eat normally you might overeat and feel fat and terrible. You may have attempted to rationalize negative thoughts but still the drive to starve is overpowering.

At this point, you need to be able quickly to stop your train of thought and realize that you do actually have a choice in your decision to starve or not; and then to distract yourself from the preoccupation with eating/not eating. Step 3 on negative automatic thoughts should have helped you to be more aware of the ways in which you think and thus make it easier to break the cycle of unhelpful thought patterns. Here we introduce the next step in the coping strategy, which will direct you away from the focus on the drive to starve.

You will need a few small cards – postcards cut in half would do well, or small index cards. What you will do is write on each one a distracting activity that you can do at any time, without preparation. Each activity should fall into one of the three categories listed below, and you should try to think of at least three activities for each category. Some people have found it useful to have different sets of cards – one set for home, and another for work etc. – as some activities (e.g. going to bed!) are not appropriate in all situations. Some examples are given here to help you.

Category 1: Things that you know are helpful, e.g.
- doing your relaxation tape
- listening to music
- going to bed

Category 2: Things that you enjoy doing, e.g.
- taking a bath
- drawing
- doing some yoga/exercise
- reading from a chapter of a novel

Category 3: Things that you must do, e.g.
- writing a letter
- housework (be specific, e.g. vacuuming)
- phoning a friend
- writing a diary

Put the cards into a box or your handbag, where you can easily get to them as you need them.

The strategy, described above, helps you to discover that you do have a choice and to find out that there are alternatives available to cope with tension and stress. This discovery also helps you to become aware that you have control over your bulimic symptoms.

Long-term Coping: A Maintenance Plan

You may by this time be feeling that you "should" be improving and beginning to reduce your anorexic symptoms, but have perhaps not been able to make any great changes in your behavior. It is normal to feel some distress at the prospect of "giving up" AN – we have seen repeatedly during this manual how it gives people a sense of control that is otherwise lacking in their lives, and how it comes to dominate life. It is difficult to replace the perceived advantages with alternative ways of coping, and you are certainly not a failure if you have not yet managed to do this.

By now you will have developed a better understanding of your AN, and so you will know that eating problems may recur at times of stress. It may be helpful to regard your eating problems as an "Achilles heel" – a vulnerable area, so that this is how you may react at times of difficulty. This does not mean you can never get better; it just means that you might have to be more aware of your reaction to stressful situations.

You will hopefully have discovered while working through this manual that certain strategies help you regain control over eating. These strategies should be re-established under two sets of circumstances:

- if you sense you are at risk of relapse, or
- if your eating problem has deteriorated.

At such times there will often be some unsolved difficulty underlying your relapse or fear of relapse. An appropriate response would therefore be twofold:

- First, examine what is happening in your life and look for any events or difficulties that might be of relevance. Once these have been identified, consider all possible solutions to these problems and construct an appropriate plan of action.

- In addition, you could use one or more of the following strategies to help you regain control over eating. Some of these will sound familiar to you, as they echo guidance given in Step 2 of this manual. You may well find it helpful to go right back to these basic points when you find yourself in difficulty.

Set some time aside to re-evaluate your progress every day or so. Some strategies may have worked; some may not. If you find that something isn't working, don't berate yourself for failure; try something else.

Additional Coping Strategies

- Recommence monitoring everything you eat, when you eat it, using the food diary format set out in Step 2.
- Try to eat in company, not alone.
- Stick to eating three or four planned meals each day, plus one or two planned snacks. Try to have these meals and snacks at predetermined times, in the sequence: breakfast, mid-morning snack, lunch, mid-afternoon snack, dinner, supper. The diet should be able to maintain a healthy weight or approach it at an appropriate rate of weight gain.
- Plan your days ahead. Avoid both long periods of unstructured time and overbooking. If you are feeling at risk of losing control, plan your meals in detail so that you know exactly what and when you will be eating. In general, you should try to keep one step ahead of the problem.
- Try to eat at least four starch-based meals/ snacks per day, and if possible five or six. Starch is better than high-sugar foods at normalizing hunger/satiety.
- Try not to eat all or most of your calories at one time. There is a tendency for calories taken over a short period of time, with long periods of fasting in between, to lead to proportionately more weight gain than calories spread evenly.
- Introduce different or new foods into your diet regularly. If this is not possible while weight is being gained, leave this

stage until weight gain has been established; but do be sure to include it!

- Try not to do anything else while you eat, except socializing – remember that meals are times of important social contact. For instance, do not watch television, do not read books or magazines. It is usually all right to listen to music or the radio, but you should try to concentrate on enjoying the meal.
- Don't weigh yourself more than once a week. Remember that fluctuations of up to 1kg (2.2 lb) either up or down are quite normal; therefore if you weigh yourself too often you may feel that you are gaining or losing weight when you are merely monitoring this daily variability. Remember that short periods of severe dieting tend to lead to transient weight loss of fluid, and similarly resuming normal eating will lead to temporary rapid weight gain.
- Remember that each time you diet and lose weight you tend to lose equal amounts of fat and muscle from your body. When you start to regain weight, initially it is nearly all fat that you put back on. This means that each time you diet, lose weight and then regain weight, the percentage of your body which is composed of fat increases.
- If you are thinking too much about your shape, ask yourself whether this is because you are anxious or depressed. You probably tend to feel fat when things are not going well. See whether you can identify any current problems and do something positive to solve or at least minimize them.
- Try not to be "phobic" about your body. Do not avoid looking in mirrors or using communal changing rooms.
- If possible, confide in someone. Explain your present predicament. A trouble shared is a trouble halved. You would not mind any friend of yours sharing his or her problems with you, would you?

Take some time just now to highlight which of these strategies are most helpful to you. When you find yourself in difficulties, or going through a relapse, try to use them before seeking professional help; remember, you have used them with benefit in the past. But if you do need further help with your eating problem, do contact your GP or local self-help group. Contact details for some organizations that could put you in touch with a local group are given on pp. 185–6.

Ways to Relax

Learning to switch off, particularly from our own thought processes, is not as easy as it sounds. It is particularly difficult for someone with AN, as these inner thoughts are very insistent and constant. However, there are many techniques for relaxation, from aromatherapy to yoga, and one of them is going to suit you. Remember, however, that worrying about not being able to relax will jeopardize your chances of any technique being effective.

Before you attempt any of these relaxation techniques, be aware of why you must give time to yourself. Many people with AN make unreasonable demands of themselves, and have little patience with what they perceive as their weaknesses. You must learn to be kinder to yourself, and to see your relaxation periods as an important part of your routine. If you fail to give yourself time to switch off, you may become very distressed and tired, and feel your motivation to change begin to diminish. Try to regard these periods as a form of battery recharging, and as essential to your progress as drinking enough water.

Aromatherapy

Aromatherapy has become incredibly popular over the last few years, and aromatherapy products are now widely available. The basic principle of aromatherapy is that the fragrances of essential oils can be used to improve health, and it has been shown to be particularly effective when dealing with stress and anxiety. Camomile and lavender oils are particularly good for treating anxiety and aiding relaxation, and blend well together. However, when using pure essential oils it is important to avoid the undiluted oils making contact with the skin; and they should *never* be taken internally.

A good way to use them is to run a warm bath and add five drops of each to the running water. Alternatively, you could buy ready-made bath oils and bubble baths, which are available from most department stores and pharmacies, and are ready formulated to treat particular conditions.

Another excellent method is to invest in an aromatherapy oil burner, which allows the scent vapours to permeate the room. If you choose this method, you will need to invest in a carrier oil, such as wheatgerm, to dilute the main oil. Add two teaspoons of carrier oil to three drops of camomile and two of juniper, which has a very clean, peaceful scent.

Oils and oil burners are available from most health shops, as are books that give further details of the properties of essential oils and how to use them. If you feel that aromatherapy is particularly suited to you, you would be well advised to consult a trained aromatherapist who can prescribe the oils that are especially suited to you and your needs. An aromatherapist will also take into consideration your lifestyle and circumstances, and the fact that you are seeking to combat AN, when prescribing treatment.

Meditation

Despite its image as the practice of bearded mystics, meditation need have no religious or cultish overtones at all. Nor does it affect normal thought processes. In face, when you are meditating, you are intensely aware of yourself and your surroundings, but in a way that might appeal to the person with AN, in that it teaches you to focus within yourself, rather than on your physical body. As you become expert in meditation, you will be able to stop the flow of negative and self-defeating thoughts that dominate your consciousness, and this can provide a tremendous feeling of release. It will also enable you to examine the way that you think in a more dispassionate way, rather than being at the mercy of it.

Being taught is the ideal way to learn this art, though it is important to find a teacher who is trained and whom you trust. Self-help guides are also available. Meditation requires 100 per cent concentration, and may be based on a visual image or a repetition of sounds or words, known as a mantra. This need have no significance other than that the sound appeals to you and induces a sense of peacefulness. Many who have learned to meditate report increased feelings of self-confidence as well as vastly reduced anxiety and susceptibility to stress. Furthermore, as you are undergoing a period of great change in your life, regular practice of meditation will help you to feel more in control of your situation and more "grounded".

Another useful feature of meditation is that, once you have mastered it, you will be able to devise "quick fixes" for yourself. For example, if you know that your anxiety levels will rise prior to a meal, even to the extent that it just seems easier to avoid the whole thing altogether, you could devise a five-minute meditation, perhaps based on an image or a mantra, that will release that anxiety and allow you to face the task ahead.

Relaxation Tapes

There are many excellent relaxation tapes available, with sound-tracks varying from whale song to spoken journeys. If you find it hard to relax and to concentrate on abstract sound, a spoken relaxation tape will probably suit you. You can buy a pre-recorded one, or you can record your own. Below is an example of a relaxation script which you can adapt to suit your tastes, or use as a springboard for creating your own. Remember to choose images and sensations that appeal to you, and that you associate with being relaxed.

Close your eyes and imagine yourself standing on a newly mown lawn on a warm summer's morning. You can feel the springy grass, still slightly wet from the dew, beneath your feet. You can feel the sun, already warm, across the back of your shoulders. Take a deep breath and suck in the smell of the grass and the sunlight on your skin. Through your closed eyelids the sunlight seems red.

As you breathe out you become aware of the sounds of birds singing in the trees, and in the far distance you can hear the hum of a lawnmower. Otherwise there is silence all around. Look around you and see that you are standing on a lawn

*before a magnificent country house. Look at the way the sun
lights up the stonework, and at the clear blue sky above it. In
the distance you can see the road leading from the house
through lush green parkland. In the far, far distance is the sea,
glittering at the horizon. Your body feels very light and clean,
and you move easily, almost without effort.*

*Take another deep breath and begin to walk away from the
house. Feel the grass under your feet give way to sun-warmed
stone, and see that you are standing at the top of a shallow
flight of stone steps. These steps lead down to an ornamental
garden. As you slowly descend them, you begin to hear the
splashing of a fountain. The sound is very cool and light, and
makes you feel refreshed.*

*As you reach the bottom step, you breathe in the fragrance of
summer flowers. All around you is vibrant – bright yellows and
violets and pinks and reds. Stems reach up from stone urns
and from flower beds. You walk along the stone-flagged paths
that surround these flower beds. Trail your fingers across the
heads of the flowers and feel the softness of the petals. Breathe
deeply. Take slow, langorous steps and allow yourself to sink
into the atmosphere. Stay as long as you like.*

*When you are ready to move on, take the right-hand path from
the garden and let it lead you through the trees. Under their
canopy it is very cool, and the noise of the water becomes louder.
As you emerge into the sunlight, you are standing in front of a
stone fountain, set in the middle of an ornamental lake. The
water rises high, and you can feel flecks of spray on your arms
and face. Take a seat beside the lake and let the spray cool
your shoulders as you turn your face to the sun. Take a deep
breath and smile. This is your own, peaceful place, and you
can stay as long as you wish.*

*When you are ready to go, return through the trees to the
garden. Feel the cool stones under your feet and smell the flowers as you pass. Climb slowly back up to the lawn. Take your
time. As you emerge from the top step you note that the sun is
higher in the sky, and the grass is warmer and drier beneath*

your feet. As you walk closer to the house, you see that the hallway looks cool and dark and inviting. Walk slowly toward the house, feeling the sun on your face. Hear the birds in the trees and the distant lawnmower, almost imperceptible now. Look up and see the faraway glitter of the sea. As you walk, get ready to say goodbye to the garden. As your feet touch the smooth flagstones of the hall floor, slowly open your eyes.

At the end of the "relaxation journey", always give yourself a couple of minutes to readjust to where you are.

If you prefer to construct your own journey, cast your mind back to a time and place where you were happy. Maybe you would prefer to imagine yourself on a beach, with the sand between your toes and the sound of the waves in your ears. Maybe you like mountains or rivers. Don't worry about creating perfectly detailed pictures in your mind's eye. The important thing is that you can, even to a small extent, sink into this imaginative landscape and recreate, in your imagination, sounds and scents. If the first time is a little disappointing, don't be discouraged. You will improve with practice. The important thing is to set aside some time, probably 15–20 minutes, every day for this exercise.

Yoga

Yoga is a wonderful way of learning to relax as it requires total concentration. It is also beneficial for the person with AN in that it helps you to develop excellent posture and muscle tone, which in turn can assist the development of a more positive body image. Ideally, you should be taught by a teacher, either individually or as part of a class. If the idea of learning such a physical art in front of others makes you feel too self-conscious, then you could try teaching yourself using a self-help guide.

As with the relaxation tape, you must find a regular slot in the day to practise and be able to do so without distraction or interruption. You will also have to be patient, as the benefits of yoga take at least a few sessions to become apparent. However, once you become adept at it, it is an excellent means of switching off from your thoughts and worries.

Other Suggestions

Gentle exercise is beneficial to relaxation, so long as it is undertaken for the purposes of winding down, rather than burning off calories. Reading can also be effective if it is done purely for enjoyment. Alternatively, you might want to consider taking up a new hobby. Try to find something that does not require vast amounts of preparation or money. Ideally, you want something which you can pick up at any point during the day. Resist the notion that it must be educational or improving in some way; this is something just for you. Even completing jigsaw puzzles might do the trick, if it is absorbing enough to distract you from worries and negative thought patterns.

Avoiding Backsliding

There is no easy solution to the problem of backsliding, that is, reverting to old ways of thinking and old routines. We noted at the very beginning of this step that it would be unrealistic to expect never to relapse. Sometimes you will feel that you have achieved nothing, and are as trapped by your AN as you were when you started trying to change. Try not to let these feelings overwhelm you, and keep to the forefront of your mind that what you are trying to achieve is not easy. The following summary points may help you to get back on track and persevere with your efforts.

Accept Rocky Progress

You may have very high expectations of yourself, and expect yourself to be able to achieve whatever you set your mind to. You *can* overcome your AN; but you may not be able to do it as quickly and smoothly as you would wish. If there are issues that you stumble over, such as that of breaking the habit of constantly weighing yourself, do not give up. Begin each stage of change, even if you are doing so for the umpteenth time, in the state of mind in which you first approached it. You will have breakthroughs, and you will make progress. The hard part is accepting that sometimes this progress will be slow, and sometimes it will seem to be non-existent.

Reverting Back to Old Ways of Thinking

Sometimes you may find yourself becoming reabsorbed into your old anorexic ways of thinking. If this happens, look back over your diary and, if necessary, work through Steps 3 and 4 again on "Challenging the Way you Think". It is hard to change the way you see things, but it is far from impossible. However, be wary of the tendency to revert out of the fear of change. You will be happier, and more in control of your life, without your AN; so resist any notion that AN is something that offers you refuge and safety.

Depression

Constant or increasing depression will hinder your attempts to change, as it will rob you of motivation and make you feel that your efforts are hopeless. If you find this to be the case, consult your GP or a counsellor, who will be able to offer advice on how to treat your depression. Don't fall into the trap of thinking that you will work on your AN once your depression has lifted. Remember that there will never be a time that seems "right" for making these difficult changes, and once you have made the commitment to change, don't let anything stand in your way.

Changes in Circumstance or Lifestyle

Many people feel very stressed by change, whether it takes the form of a new job, a new member of the family, or a move of house. In such situations, we often reach out for the familiar, clinging to old routines and behaviors, and in most cases this is a harmless part of the readjustment process. However, for the person with AN, it is not harmless, and could be the beginning of your sliding back into the grip of the disease. Be kind to yourself, and aware that lifestyle changes are stressful for everyone. Keep going with your efforts; remember that being free from AN will leave you much better equipped to cope with life events, including further changes of circumstance, in the future.

A Final Word

The model for treatment contained in this book has proved to be a successful one, and I hope that by the time you read this, it is proving to be successful for you too. However, if it is not, this does not mean that your case is untreatable, and the very fact that you have persisted thus far proves that your case is far from hopeless. If you feel that you are back at square one, or have made a small step in the right direction but find yourself unable to move any further, now is the time to seek professional help.

Your first step may be your GP or family doctor. If you feel that your doctor is unable to help you, ask to be referred to a specialist, or contact an organization such as Overeaters Anonymous or the national Eating Disorders Association, contact details for which are given on pp. 185–6. They will be able to offer advice and put you in touch with groups and specialists in your area.

It is very important that you do not become discouraged. Try to take each day as it comes, and count your successes, not your failures. Enlist support from friends and family, and maintain awareness of your situation, your state of mind and your physical health. And remember that many, many thousands of men and women have been in just such circumstances as yours, and have recovered and gone on to lead fulfilling and happy lives. You can do that too.

Useful Books

Gillian Butler, *Overcoming Social Anxiety and Shyness* (Robinson, 1999 and NYUP, 2001)

Peter J. Cooper, *Bulimia Nervosa and Binge-Eating: A Guide to Recovery* (Robinson, 1995 and NYUP, 1995)

Melanie Fennell, *Overcoming Low Self-Esteem* (Robinson, 1999 and NYUP, 2001)

Paul Gilbert, *Overcoming Depression* (Robinson, 2000 and O.U.P., 2001)

Helen Kennerley, *Overcoming Anxiety* (Robinson, 1997 and NYUP, 1997)

Derrick Silove and Vijaya Manicavagasar, *Overcoming Panic* (Robinson, 1997 and NYUP, 2001)

Manuel J. Smith, *When I Say No, I Feel Guilty* (Bantam Books, 1975)

Useful Addresses

Eating Disorders Association
Head Office
Sackville Place
44 Magdalen Street
Norwich
Norfolk NR3 1JU

Tel. helpline: 01603 621414

Overeaters Anonymous
PO Box 19
Stretford
Manchester M32 9EB

Tel. 07626 984674

Scottish Association for Mental Health
Atlantic House
38 Gardners Crescent
Edinburgh EH3 8DQ

Tel. 0131 229 9687

Health Education Board for Scotland (HEBS)
Woodburn House
Canaan Lane
Edinburgh EH10 4SG

Tel. 0345 708010

Priory Hospitals Limited (specialists in the treatment of eating disorders)
Broadwater Park
Denham
Uxbridge
Middlesex UB9 5HP

Tel. 01895 836311

USA

Overeaters Anonymous
World Service Office
6075 Zenith Ct. NE
Rio Rancho, NM 87124

National Association of Anorexia Nervosa and Associated Disorders (ANAD)
PO Box 7
Highland Park
IL 60035

Index

addiction, concept of 2, 32
adolescence 10, 34, 41, 53, 57–8, 59, 60, 61, 64, 66, 67, 81
agoraphobia 38–9
alcohol 17, 32, 62, 108
amenorrhea 9, 17, 23, 24, 41, 47, 49
anaemia 17
anorexia nervosa
    abstinent AN 31, 32, 33
    age of onset 9
    behavioral effects 13–14, 25–6
    bulimic AN 31–3, 67, 92
    causes 11, 51–68
    "clinical AN" 90
    diagnosis 40, 42–4, 71–2
    and dieting distinguished 12–14, 44–5
    fatal outcomes 10, 11, 15
    gender and 9, 10, 11, 40
    incidence of 10, 14, 40
    late onset AN 49–50
    myths concerning 11–12
    personal experiences 5–6, 32, 36, 37, 61, 87, 102–3, 132, 150–1, 154, 169
    physical effects 9, 16–25
    population groups and 40–50
    "pre-anorexia nervosa" 90
    pros and cons of AN 94–6
    and psychological disorders 33–9
    psychological effects 26–30
    recovery 12, 24, 69
    "reverse" AN 48–9
    social groups and 9, 11
    symptoms 9, 17–18
    treatment 69–84
    as a weapon 63, 100–1
anti-psychotic drugs 79
antidepressants 46, 79–80, 92
anxiety disorders 17, 27, 38–9, 50, 79, 108, 154–60
    dealing with 154–60
    and eating 158

effects on thought patterns 156–7
relationship with AN 38–9
relaxation techniques 158–60, 174–9
symptoms 154–7
appetite loss 43–4, 64
art therapy 73–4
assertiveness 80–1
    aggression 142, 143, 144, 147, 152
    assertive behavior 142, 144, 147–51, 152
    "assertiveness rights" 141–2
    confrontative assertion 149
    developing 141–53
    empathic assertion 148
    escalating assertion 149
    I-language assertion 149
    non-assertion 142, 143, 144, 147, 151–2
automatic thoughts
    challenging 110–18
    characteristics of 114
    negative thoughts 82, 83, 114, 115, 117, 121, 122, 169, 170
    recording 115, 116
    thoughts, mood and behavior cycle 82–3, 110–11, 114, 117
    typical anorexic thoughts 112–13, 115, 117
    understanding 113–15
    see also thinking errors

Beck, Aaron T. xii, 81
behavior therapy xi, xii
behavioral effects of AN 13–14, 25–6
binge eating 10, 31, 32, 41, 47, 64, 67
    features 10
    incidence of 10
biological factors 54–5
black-and-white thinking 29, 119
blood pressure, low 20, 21
body image
    appearance, disgust with 38
    body image activities 136–8
    creating an alternative image 135

Index

distortion of 9, 14, 48, 68, 74, 131–3, 138, 139
ideal and reality 58–9, 133–4
improving 131–40
"reverse" AN 48–9
writing your body's history 134–6
body mass index 75, 192–4
brain shrinkage 17, 18, 21, 24
bulimia nervosa (BN) 10, 26, 64, 67
bulimic AN 31–3, 67, 92
children and 43
features 10
incidence of 10, 14

calcium deficiency 19, 22
cardiomyopathy 21
causes of AN 11, 51–68
maintaining factors 52, 66–8, 90
triggering factors 48, 52, 66, 90, 107–8
vulnerability factors 51–65
change
commitment to 92–3
fear of 93, 180
inability to cope with 65, 66
obstacles to 92–4
chest pains 17
children, AN in 40–7, 64–5, 73
adolescent crisis 57–8
autonomy, search for 60–1
diagnosis 40, 42–4
early feeding patterns 52–4
early warning signs 44–5
features 41
long-term repercussions 41
physical complications 41–2, 47
pre-pubescent children 19, 40, 44, 45, 46, 73
psychological complications 42, 47
schooling 42
social/familial complications 42
treatment 46–7, 73
chloropromazine 79
cholecystokinin (CCK) 55
clinical psychology 72
cognitive behavioral therapy xii–xiv, 72–3, 81–4
see also automatic thoughts; thinking errors
cognitive impairment 18, 27
cold, sensitivity to 17, 22–3
concealment of food 14, 45, 76
concentration, poor 27
constipation 17, 22, 24, 26, 71
control
exercising 10, 26, 32, 42, 44, 50, 58, 63, 67, 139, 166–7, 169
loss of 10, 28, 63, 76, 93, 167

coping strategies 169–80
activity cards 170–1
crisis moments 169–71
maintenance plan 171–4
relaxation 158–60, 174–9
counselling 46, 70, 72–3, 74, 81
family counselling 46, 81
parental counselling 46

death rates 10, 11, 15
dehydration 18, 20, 24, 26, 41, 47
denial and deception 13, 45, 49, 69
dental damage 17, 23, 24
depression xiii, 17, 26, 33–5, 49, 50, 64, 71, 75, 77, 79–80, 92, 108, 111, 180
in children 41, 42, 43–4, 45, 46, 47, 64–5
features 33
relationship with AN 33–5
diabetes 75
diagnosis of AN 40, 42–4, 71–2
diarrhoea 17
dietary treatment 46–7, 73, 80
dieting 11, 34, 47, 50, 66, 90, 139, 173
and AN distinguished 12–14, 44–5
diuretic abuse 26
dizziness and faintness 17, 21, 23
drug abuse 32, 44, 48
drug treatment 46, 72, 75, 79–80

eating
lingering over food 14, 28
monitoring 104–9
in public 14, 38
ritualization of 14, 27–8, 45
selective eating 43
eating patterns
changing 75, 106–7, 123–30, 172–3
portion system 46, 127–9, 130
elderly people 49–50
emotional abuse 57
emotional instability 27, 32
endocrine disorder 44
energy levels 23, 55, 126
epileptic seizures 18, 19
euphoria 5, 34
exercise 6, 9, 12, 25, 26, 45, 47, 67, 108, 138

families and AN 11, 42, 46, 98–101
autonomy, desire for 60–1
family dynamics 42, 55–8, 66, 100–1
genetic predisposition to AN 54
myths concerning 11
parents with eating disorders 53–4
positive and negative aspects of recovery 99
self-blame 42
siblings 42, 56–7, 60–1, 101
support for an action plan 99–100

Index

family counselling 46, 81
family therapy 46, 74, 81, 101
fatigue and weakness 17, 19, 26
fatness, fear of 9, 14, 47, 49, 53, 67
fertility, impaired 17, 24, 41
food
    preoccupation with 13, 14, 27–8, 90, 108
    refusal, fads and fetishes 28, 43, 48, 58, 60
    see also eating
Food Avoidance Emotional Disorder
    (FAED) 43
food diaries 73, 104–6, 109
food supplements 46–7
future, projecting into the 95, 97, 136–7

gastro-intestinal problems 18, 22
general practitioners (GPs) 71
genetic predisposition 54
glycogen stores 124, 125, 126, 129
group therapy 80–1
growth impairment 41
guilt and self-disgust 2, 31, 32, 63
gums, bleeding 18

hair
    dry hair 17
    hair loss 17
    lanugo 17, 20
heart problems 16, 17, 18, 20, 21, 26
heartburn 17, 23
hospitalization 42, 47, 75–8
hyperactivity 25, 37, 45
hyperventilation 155, 156
hypoglycaemia 15
hypothermia 15, 18, 22

immune system impairment 17, 22
inflammatory bowel disease 44
isolation 26, 29, 30, 94

kidney damage 16, 17, 18, 21–2

lanugo 17, 20
laxative abuse 10, 24, 26, 31, 41, 47
lazy bowel syndrome 24
life events, significant 48, 50, 180
lips, cracked 17
low back pain 21

magnesium deficiency 20
memory impairment 27
men with AN 2, 11, 40, 47–9
    body-builders 48–9
    common features 48
    symptoms 47
menstruation 6, 9, 19, 24, 92, 108
    cessation of 9, 17, 19, 23, 24, 41, 47, 49,
       71, 92
metabolic rates 17, 19, 22, 126–7, 129–30

mineral deficiency 19–20
miscarriage 23
mood swings 26
multifollicular ovaries 18
muscle tremors 18, 20
muscle wasting and weakness 17, 20–1
myopathy 20–1

obsessional disorders 30, 36–8, 45
    features 36
    relationship with AN 36–8
obsessionality 14, 30, 48, 75, 91, 108
occupational therapy 74
orange palms/yellow skin 17, 20
osteoporosis 16, 17, 19–20, 21, 41–2
ovary and uterus shrinkage 17, 23

panic attacks 39, 157
parental counselling 46
percutaneous endoscopic gastroscopy 77
perfectionism 50, 133, 134, 139
personality type 65, 66
Pervasive Refusal Syndrome 43
physical abuse 56
physical effects of anorexia nervosa 9, 16–
    25
polycystic ovaries 18
potassium deficiency 18, 20, 22, 23, 26
psychiatry 72
psychoanalysis xi
psychoeducational therapy 80
psychological disorders 17, 33–9
psychological effects of AN 26–30
psychotherapy xi, 46, 72, 74
puberty 19, 41, 66
purging 9, 10, 23–4, 25–6, 32, 43, 64, 67,
    75
    see also diuretic abuse; laxative abuse;
      vomiting
purpura (easy bruising) 18

refeeding programmes 46, 77–8
regressive behavior 42
relationships
    AN and 29, 53, 66, 101–3
    changing 166–7
    examining 164–5
    interpersonal maps 161–4
    managing 161–8
    supportive 166
    see also families and AN
relaxation 158–60, 174–9
    aromatherapy 174–5
    meditation 175–6
    relaxation tapes 158, 176–8
    yoga 178
reproductive system 17, 23, 24

Index

self-esteem, low 14, 26, 42, 53, 61–2, 65, 66, 77, 80, 152
self-harm 32, 75
self-help 2, 87–180
  assertiveness, developing 141–53
  assessing the problem 89–99
  awareness of obstacles 92–4
  backsliding, dealing with 179–80
  body image, improving 131–40
  coping strategies 169–80
  dealing with anxiety 154–60
  diary keeping 89, 93, 104–6, 109, 115, 116, 121, 136
  eating, monitoring 104–9
  eating patterns, changing 123–30
  and family relationships 98–101
  helpful tactics 107–8
  recognizing benefits of change 87–8
  relationships, managing 161–8
  relaxation 158–60, 174–9
  seeking professional help 2, 70, 91–2, 181
  self-defeating mechanisms 94
  writing a letter to your AN 97–8
self-help groups 71
self-help manuals xiv
separation and loss, dealing with 50, 64–5
serotonin 55
sexual abuse 56, 62–3
sexuality/sexual relations 27, 50, 57, 88, 101, 102
"sick role" 67, 76, 99
skin discoloration 17, 20
skin problems 17, 20
social anxiety 38
social class, AN and 9, 11
social pressure to be slim 49, 58–60, 135–6
social skills training 80
sodium deficiency 20
starvation 9, 10, 31, 34, 41, 49, 54–5, 64, 67, 74, 80
  physical and psychological effects 16–30, 74, 126–7
stomach ulcers 18, 23
suicide 10, 15, 32, 75
support groups 94
swollen ankles/puffy hands 17, 18

tetany 18, 20
thinking, disturbed 26–30, 111–13
  effects of anxiety disorders 156–7
  immature thinking 29
  obsessionality 14, 30, 48, 75, 108
  rigid thinking processes 29, 47
  stereotyped thinking and behavior 30

thinking errors 119–22, 133
  and body image distortion 133
  common errors 119–20
  see also automatic thoughts
throat, sore 17, 23
total parenteral hyperalimentation 77–8
tranquillizers 79
treatment 69–84
  art therapy 73–4
  of children 46–7, 73
  clinical psychology 72
  cognitive behavioral therapy xii–xiv, 72–3, 81–4
  counselling 46, 72–3, 74, 81
  dietary treatment 46–7, 73, 80
  drug treatment 46, 72, 75, 79–80
  general practitioners (GPs) 71
  group therapy 80–1
  hospitalization 42, 47, 75–8
  initial steps 70
  involuntary treatment 78
  occupational therapy 74
  outpatient treatment 70, 78–9
  physicians 71–2
  principles and objectives 74–5
  psychiatry 72
  psychotherapy 46, 72
  specialist services 70–4
triggering factors 48, 52, 66, 90, 107–8
twins 54

vegan and vegetarian diets 28
vitamin deficiencies 18
vitamin supplements 46
vomiting 9, 10, 17, 19, 23, 26, 31, 32, 43, 45, 47, 76
vulnerability factors 51–65
  adolescent crisis 57–8
  autonomy, search for 60–1
  biological factors 54–5
  early feeding patterns 52–4
  family structure 55–7
  genetic predisposition 54
  self-esteem, low 61–2, 65
  separation and loss 64–5
  sexual abuse 62–3
  social pressure to be slim 49, 58–60

water retention and bloating 24, 26
weighing oneself 5, 6, 108, 173
weight fluctuations 123–6, 129
weight gain 16, 24, 74, 123, 129, 173
withdrawal behavior 67

Body Mass Index Charts

The chart on the next page can be used to determine your body mass index (BMI) and is applicable to both men and women, at any age. Once you have found your BMI on the first graph, there are two subsequent graphs plotting the full BMI range, one for boys and one for girls, with "at risk" levels shown as shaded areas. Between the ages of 0 and 20 the graph is curved, to take into account the growth rates and growth spurts that naturally occur at different ages. It is important to remember that weight gain is usual up until the late teens, and that staying the same weight for prolonged periods during these years is equivalent to losing weight once growth has stopped. At around 20 years of age the graph will plateau, so this level should be used to determine your potential risk status from that age onwards.

Body Mass Index Reckoner (BMI)

Pounds		1.36	1.40	1.44	1.48	1.52	1.56	1.60	1.64	1.68	1.72	1.76	1.80	1.84	1.88	1.92	1.96	2.00	Kilograms
168		41	39	37	35	33	31	30	28	27	26	25	23	22	22	21	20	19	76
		41	38	36	34	32	31	29	28	27	25	24	23	22	21	20	20	19	75
		40	38	36	34	32	30	29	28	26	25	24	23	22	21	20	19	19	74
161		39	37	35	33	32	30	29	27	26	25	24	23	22	21	20	19	18	73
		39	37	35	33	31	30	28	27	26	24	23	22	21	20	20	19	18	72
		38	36	34	32	31	29	28	26	25	24	23	22	21	20	19	18	18	71
154		38	36	34	32	30	29	27	26	25	24	23	22	21	20	19	18	18	70
		37	35	33	32	30	28	27	26	24	23	22	21	20	20	19	18	17	69
		37	35	33	31	29	28	27	25	24	23	22	21	20	19	18	18	17	68
147		36	34	32	31	29	28	26	25	24	23	22	21	20	19	18	17	17	67
		36	34	32	30	29	27	26	25	23	22	21	20	20	19	18	17	17	66
		35	33	31	30	28	27	25	24	23	22	21	20	19	18	18	17	16	65
140		35	33	31	29	28	26	25	24	23	22	21	20	19	18	17	17	16	64
		34	32	30	29	27	26	25	23	22	21	20	19	19	18	17	16	16	63
		34	32	30	28	27	25	24	23	22	21	20	19	18	18	17	16	16	62
		33	31	29	28	26	25	24	23	22	21	20	19	18	17	17	16	15	61
		32	31	29	27	26	25	23	22	21	20	19	19	18	17	16	16	15	60
		32	30	28	27	26	24	23	22	21	20	19	18	17	17	16	15	15	59
126		31	30	28	26	25	24	23	22	21	20	19	18	17	16	16	15	15	58
		31	29	27	26	25	23	22	21	20	19	18	18	17	16	15	15	14	57
		30	29	27	26	24	23	22	21	20	19	18	17	17	16	15	15	14	56
119		30	28	27	25	24	23	21	20	19	19	18	17	16	16	15	14	14	55
		29	28	26	25	23	22	21	20	19	18	17	17	16	15	15	14	14	54
		29	27	26	24	23	22	21	20	19	18	17	16	16	15	14	14	13	53
112		28	27	25	24	23	21	20	19	18	18	17	16	15	15	14	14	13	52
		28	26	25	23	22	21	20	19	18	17	16	16	15	14	14	13	13	51
		27	26	24	23	22	21	20	19	18	17	16	15	15	14	14	13	13	50
105		26	25	24	22	21	20	19	18	17	17	16	15	14	14	13	13	12	49
		26	24	23	22	21	20	19	18	17	16	16	15	14	14	13	12	12	48
		25	24	23	21	20	19	18	17	17	16	15	15	14	13	13	12	12	47
98		25	23	22	21	20	19	18	17	16	16	15	14	14	13	12	12	12	46
		24	23	22	21	19	18	18	17	16	15	15	14	13	13	12	12	11	45
		24	22	21	20	19	18	17	16	16	15	14	14	13	12	12	11	11	44
		23	22	21	20	19	18	17	16	15	15	14	13	13	12	12	11	11	43
91		23	21	20	19	18	17	16	16	15	14	14	13	12	12	11	11	11	42
		22	21	20	19	18	17	16	15	15	14	13	13	12	12	11	11	10	41
		22	20	19	18	17	16	16	15	14	14	13	12	12	11	11	10	10	40
		21	20	19	18	17	16	15	15	14	13	13	12	12	11	11	10	10	39
		21	19	18	17	16	16	15	14	13	13	12	12	11	11	10	10	10	38
		20	19	18	17	16	15	14	14	13	13	12	11	11	10	10	10	09	37
		19	18	17	16	16	15	14	13	13	12	12	11	11	10	10	09	09	36
77		19	18	17	16	15	14	14	13	12	12	11	11	10	10	09	09	09	35
		18	17	16	16	15	14	13	13	12	11	11	10	10	10	09	09	09	34
		18	17	16	15	14	14	13	12	12	11	11	10	10	09	09	09	08	33
70		17	16	15	15	14	13	13	12	11	11	10	10	09	09	09	08	08	32
		17	16	15	14	13	13	12	12	11	10	10	10	09	09	08	08	08	31
		16	15	14	14	13	12	12	11	11	10	10	09	09	08	08	08	08	30
63		16	15	14	13	13	12	11	11	10	10	09	09	09	08	08	08	07	29
		15	14	14	13	12	12	11	10	10	09	09	09	08	08	08	07	07	28
		15	14	13	12	12	11	11	10	10	09	09	08	08	08	07	07	07	27
		14	13	13	12	11	11	10	10	09	09	08	08	08	07	07	07	07	26
56		14	13	12	11	11	10	10	09	09	08	08	08	07	07	07	07	06	25
		13	12	12	11	10	10	09	09	09	08	08	07	07	07	07	06	06	24
		12	12	11	11	10	09	09	09	08	08	07	07	07	07	06	06	06	23
49		12	11	11	10	10	09	09	08	08	07	07	07	07	06	06	06	06	22
		11	11	10	10	09	09	08	08	07	07	07	06	06	06	06	05	05	21
42		11	10	10	09	09	08	08	07	07	07	06	06	06	06	05	05	05	20

HEIGHT (metres) — column headings above

HEIGHT (feet and inches): 4'6" 7" 8" 9" 10" 11" 5'0" 1" 2" 3" 4" 5" 6" 7" 8" 9" 10" 11" 6'0" 1" 2" 3" 4" 5" 6" 7"

BMI Chart for Girls From Birth to 20 Years

Work out your BMI from the chart on page 192, and check below to see where your rating falls.

A girl should be considered for referral if her BMI falls above the 99.6[th] centile (significantly overweight) or below the 0.4[th] centile (significantly underweight). It is also possible that a girl whose BMI falls in the tinted areas should also be referred.

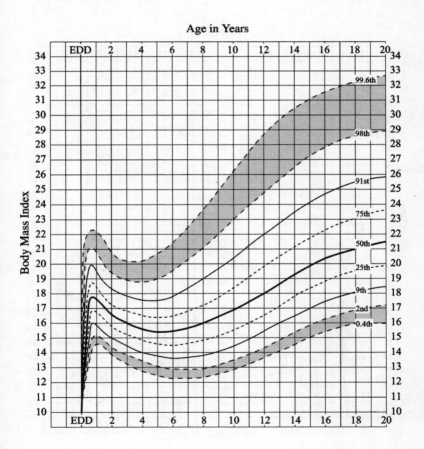

BMI Chart for Boys From Birth to 20 Years

Work out your BMI from the chart on page 192, and check below to see where your rating falls.

A boy should be considered for referral if his BMI falls above the 99.6[th] centile (significantly overweight) or below the 0.4[th] centile (significantly underweight). It is also possible that a boy whose BMI falls in the tinted areas should also be referred.

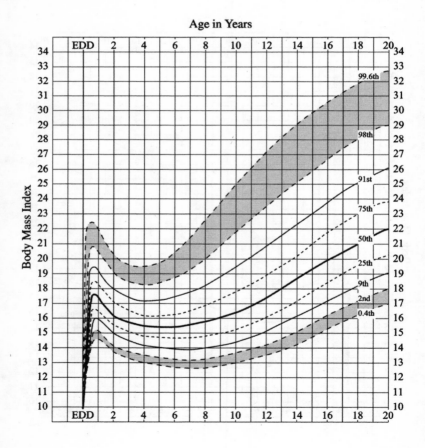

Extra Monitoring Sheets

Diary 1: Monitoring Your Eating

Date: _____   Day: _____

	Por	Vom	Lax	Ex
Breakfast				
Snack				
Lunch				
Snack				
Evening Meal				
Snack				
Totals				

Diary 1: *Monitoring Your Eating*

Date: _____   Day: _____

	Por	Vom	Lax	Ex
Breakfast				
Snack				
Lunch				
Snack				
Evening Meal				
Snack				
Totals				

Diary 1: Monitoring Your Eating

Date: _____   Day: _____

	Por	Vom	Lax	Ex
Breakfast				
Snack				
Lunch				
Snack				
Evening Meal				
Snack				
Totals				

Diary 1: Monitoring Your Eating

Date: _____   Day: _____

	Por	Vom	Lax	Ex
Breakfast				
Snack				
Lunch				
Snack				
Evening Meal				
Snack				
Totals				

Diary 1: Monitoring Your Eating

Date: _____   Day: _____

	Por	Vom	Lax	Ex
Breakfast				
Snack				
Lunch				
Snack				
Evening Meal				
Snack				
Totals				

Diary 1: Monitoring Your Eating

Date: _____   Day: _____

	Por	Vom	Lax	Ex
Breakfast				
Snack				
Lunch				
Snack				
Evening Meal				
Snack				
Totals				

Diary 1: Monitoring Your Eating

Date: _____   Day: _____

	Por	Vom	Lax	Ex
Breakfast				
Snack				
Lunch				
Snack				
Evening Meal				
Snack				
Totals				

Diary 2/3: Challenging Automatic Thoughts and Thinking Errors

Date	Emotions	Situation	Automatic thoughts	Thinking errors

Diary 2/3: Challenging Automatic Thoughts and Thinking Errors

Date	Emotions	Situation	Automatic thoughts	Thinking errors

Diary 2/3: Challenging Automatic Thoughts and Thinking Errors

Date	Emotions	Situation	Automatic thoughts	Thinking errors

Diary 2/3: Challenging Automatic Thoughts and Thinking Errors

Date	Emotions	Situation	Automatic thoughts	Thinking errors

Diary 2/3: Challenging Automatic Thoughts and Thinking Errors

Date	Emotions	Situation	Automatic thoughts	Thinking errors

Diary 2/3: Challenging Automatic Thoughts and Thinking Errors

Date	Emotions	Situation	Automatic thoughts	Thinking errors

Diary 2/3: Challenging Automatic Thoughts and Thinking Errors

Date	Emotions	Situation	Automatic thoughts	Thinking errors